Bonjour, Y'all!

Heidi's **FUSION COOKING** on the
SOUTH CAROLINA COAST

HEIDI VUKOV & SARA SOBOTA

PHOTOGRAPHS BY SCOTT SMALLIN

GIBBS SMITH
TO ENRICH AND INSPIRE HUMANKIND

First Edition
19 18 17   5 4 3 2

Published by
Gibbs Smith
P.O. Box 667
Layton, Utah 84041

1.800.835.4993 orders
www.gibbs-smith.com

Design by Katie Jennings Design
Printed and bound in Hong Kong
Gibbs Smith books are printed on either recycled, 100% post-consumer waste,
FSC-certified papers or on paper produced from sustainable PEFC-certified
forest/controlled wood source. Learn more at www.pefc.org.

Library of Congress Cataloging-in-Publication Data

Vukov, Heidi.
  Bonjour, y'all! : Heidi's fusion cooking on the South Carolina coast / Heidi
Vukov and Sara Sobota ; photographs by Scott Smallin. – First edition.
    pages cm
  Includes index.
  ISBN 978-1-4236-3994-7
  1. Cooking, American—Southern style. 2. Cooking—South Carolina.
  I. Sobota, Sara. II. Title.
  TX715.2.S68V85 2015
  641.5975—dc23
                2014044236

THIS BOOK IS DEDICATED TO MY HUSBAND, GARY, AND OUR CHILDREN, MATT, BRYAN, ALEX, AND BEN, FOR THEIR UNDERSTANDING THAT WE DID NOT HAVE TRADITIONAL WEEKENDS AND HOLIDAYS LIKE MOST FAMILIES, KNOWING THAT THOSE TIMES WERE ABOUT SERVING OTHERS FIRST. ALTHOUGH THE DAYS BEFORE THANKSGIVING AND CHRISTMAS WERE ALWAYS THE BUSIEST DAYS IN THE RESTAURANT, WE, AS A FAMILY, WERE STILL ABLE TO PULL OFF AN ENJOYABLE MEAL TO SHARE TOGETHER AND MAKE WONDERFUL MEMORIES. —*HV*

TO MY HUSBAND, CHRIS, FOR ENDURING THE HOURS I SPENT HUDDLED OVER THE COMPUTER MUMBLING ABOUT CRAB, RYE BREAD, AND PASTRIES; FOR HIS LOVE OF FOOD; AND FOR HIS SUPPORT OF MY WRITING. ALSO TO OUR BOYS, BRYCE, ALEX, AND AIDAN, WHO BECAME QUITE FOND OF THE FREQUENT TRIPS TO "HEIDI'S," WHERE THEY ALWAYS ENJOYED A SPECIAL TREAT. —*SS*

CONTENTS

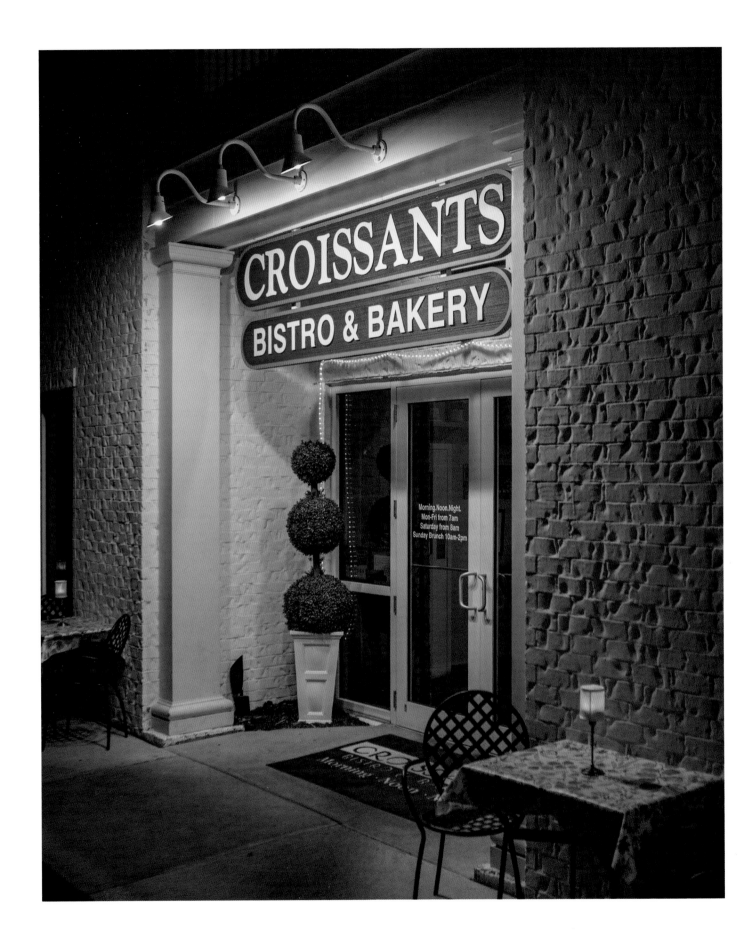

History of CROISSANTS BISTRO & BAKERY

"Bonjour, y'all!" This popular slogan for Croissants Bistro & Bakery in Myrtle Beach, South Carolina, encapsulates an unlikely pairing of two distinct culinary traditions. European cuisine and Southern home cooking seem at first to be strange bedfellows—are they serving coq au vin or biscuits and gravy?—yet diners quickly discover how this restaurant blends the best of both cultures to a savory union. Delights such as crab beignets, gazpacho with shrimp, and fruit-filled crepes reflect Croissants' success in combining the elegance and finesse of the French palate with the hospitality and warmth of the Southern kitchen. Throw in an award-winning European bakery, where gorgeous wedding cakes dot the shelves and delicate pastries fill the cases, and you've got Croissants.

So how did this fusion fare evolve? The answer lies in the creative vision of Heidi Vukov, owner and operator of Croissants. The Pennsylvania native traveled south in 1992 with the intention of making Myrtle Beach her home, and she never looked back. Her twenty-year-old restaurant is a study in experimentation, inspiration, and passion for food, and its journey has in many ways paralleled the evolution of the Myrtle Beach area itself. Heidi's knowledge of and enthusiasm for ingredients and their innovative preparation is matched only by her love for the lowcountry lifestyle and the people of the South Carolina coast. Croissants has progressed through multiple manifestations over the years—a ladies' lunch spot, a European bakery, a fusion bistro—and in each stage of the restaurant's history, Heidi has offered a dining experience that's just a little bit different . . . surprising, elegant, delicious.

In the typical combination of business acumen and serendipity that has marked the progress of her restaurant, Heidi embarked on a new mission in 2009 to sharpen Croissants' focus on lowcountry and European fusion fare. Over the subsequent five years, the restaurant has won honors including the 2011 South Carolina Restaurateur of the Year award, the Wine Spectator Award of Excellence, and the Myrtle Beach Area Chamber of Commerce awards for Small Business of the Year and Business Innovation. In a perfect pairing of homage to traditional European and Southern cuisine with an eye toward eclectic, homegrown twists and tastes, Croissants' menu and ambiance reflects Heidi's intention to take the Myrtle Beach bistro into the next culinary dimension.

This book, then, is a celebration of diversity in cooking. The recipes demonstrate how a time-honored ingredient can be shaken up a bit, paired with a new taste, and enhanced with a different cooking style. The dishes reflect a sincere respect for the land and sea of the lowcountry with a nod to European tradition, and they offer a peek into Heidi's mind, heart, and palate.

It's time now to throw open the French doors, walk out on the verandah, and find out exactly what she's got cooking.

A TASTE OF THE OLD COUNTRY

Heidi's talent and passion for baking originated in the roots of her family's history. Her father emigrated from Germany as a young man, leaving his family behind, to come to America, where he would marry and start his own family. As a young girl, Heidi traveled to Germany often, where she would accompany her grandmother on morning trips to bakeries and pastry shops. In the afternoon, Oma would make fancy desserts for afternoon tea such as fruit tarts, Black Forest Torte, or chocolate rolls. Heidi also traveled with relatives through France and Austria, sampling the beautiful desserts and experiencing baking and preparation methods firsthand. It was through her

European childhood experiences that Heidi fell in love with the art of pastry.

Meanwhile, on the other side of the pond, baking was just as rewarding and exciting in the kitchens of her American relatives. Heidi's grandmother in rural Pennsylvania, who had endured the Great Depression, taught Heidi economy and resourcefulness in baking as she churned out fruit pies and chocolate cakes with fluffy icing using local, homegrown ingredients. "We never wasted anything in our baking process," Heidi says. "We used what we had—seasonal fruits, fresh butter—and treated those ingredients with respect, because there was no going to the store to get more."

The diversity in baking styles became the foundation for Heidi's talent and creativity in the kitchen.

A RISKY MOVE

Heidi left her home in Pennsylvania and headed to Myrtle Beach in 1992, spurred by a love of the ocean and the lowcountry lifestyle. It was a romantic move in some ways—she pictured daily beach walks and serene sunrises—yet Heidi also brought with her a clear vision for her future and an ambitious business plan. In the early 1990s, Myrtle Beach was a popular regional tourist destination, but it hadn't achieved the national spotlight; no chain restaurants had arrived, and most dining spots were family run, offering traditional Southern fare. Recognizing the area's growing popularity, Heidi speculated that Myrtle Beach was ripe with potential for culinary growth. In this land of buttermilk biscuits and pancake houses, she envisioned a European café and bakery where people would surrender their grits in favor of a savory cheese Danish.

But doubts materialized during Heidi's first months in town. Though she was a highly talented baker and an aspiring entrepreneur, she was also a single mom with two kids in a small Southern area. Who, she wondered, would want to invest in a newly relocated female (from the North!) with so little established success?

In typical fashion, Heidi gregariously took to the streets, meeting locals, making friends, and establishing connections with the movers and shakers. She was eventually directed toward the more speculative and innovative of investors and, to Heidi's surprise, her first contact took a chance on the European Yankee baker. One contract and one staggering loan later, Croissants was on its way to existence.

THE OPENING DAY THAT ALMOST WASN'T

After months of preparation, hard work, and worry, Heidi spent the final day before Croissants' grand opening with her five staff members, checking off items on the comprehensive to-do list. Feeling fairly confident and organized in her final hours before officially becoming a restaurant owner, she worked through the preparatory stocking, baking, chopping, and storing tasks with her employees; then she sent them home to get some rest before the big day. Heidi stayed behind to finish up a few details and ensure that everything was ready.

That's when the troubles began. While chopping macadamia nuts for one last batch of cookies, Heidi cut her finger and, realizing it was fairly deep, quickly wrapped it in a towel to stop the bleeding. In the meantime, the dishwasher sprung a leak and water began gushing all over the floor of her new kitchen. When the water reached four inches and Heidi was standing helplessly in the middle of it, still trying to elevate her bleeding finger, she called the plumber, who headed over right away. As if on cue, the

four-foot-tall, four-hundred-pound Hobart floor mixer, the center of the baker's universe, started emitting black goo onto the waterlogged floor. "When the plumber arrived, I'm sure he felt like he'd stepped into *The Amityville Horror*," Heidi recalls. At that point, Heidi began to wonder if she should give up on this restaurant dream before it even got started.

After many hours of panic, despair, repairs, and regrouping, Heidi left the restaurant at 2 a.m., only to return at 4 a.m. to begin preparatory baking for the official opening. Such was the final challenge from the restaurant deities to test her resolve in this risky restaurant adventure.

Bleary eyed but still chock full of charm, Heidi opened the doors that morning to a modest line of guests ready to check out the area's newest café. In her thirty-five-seat establishment, she served more than a hundred people that first day, scurrying to tables to greet guests, learn faces, make connections, and ensure that everyone felt welcome. Even on that first day, she knew that locals—with their word-of-mouth chatter—could make or break a small restaurant in a tourist town. As the pastry cases emptied and the employees hustled to ring up purchases and clean tables, Croissants was making its very first mark on the Myrtle Beach community. Eleven hours and scores of guests later, an exhausted and exhilarated Heidi locked the door at 4 p.m. and turned toward the kitchen to start the cleaning process.

But it wasn't over. A friendly couple tapped on the door, pointed to the closed sign, and signaled that they wished to enter. "I was so tired, so I told them—rather rudely, I think—that we were closed," Heidi says. It was the restaurateur's first true test: did she have the endurance to offer up true Southern hospitality? "They kept standing there, so I finally let them in," Heidi continues. "They just wanted a loaf of freshly baked French bread, and I ended up chatting with them for half an hour." In this last of the day's innumerable gestures of accommodation and graciousness, Croissants established its Southern charm on the very first shift.

FIRST GENERATION

Heidi's original conception for Croissants was a bakery and pastry shop; she decided to offer breakfast and lunch items only in the last two months before opening. "When I lived in Philadelphia, there was a bakery shop on every corner," Heidi explains, "but when I came to Myrtle Beach, there was only one other bakery in town. I got too nervous to open a place that sold just desserts and baked goods, so I decided to broaden the concept so it became a café and bakery. Thank God I did, because in the beginning we were serving 90 percent savory food [breakfast and lunch items] and only 10 percent bakery."

Word of Croissants' unique, high-quality food and warm atmosphere did indeed spread throughout the Myrtle Beach community. The café became a hub for morning diners, some of whom had migrated from the North themselves and missed the Danish pastries of their youth. The younger business crowd discovered the new restaurant as well and began patronizing the café as an alternative to the area's typical pancake houses. And at lunchtime, the crowds swelled. The daily quiche specials, homemade shrimp salad, and creative sandwiches on homemade French bread were items that just couldn't be found anywhere else, and they attracted the ladies' lunch crowd as well as business luncheons.

Cautiously optimistic that this crazy restaurant idea might actually have staying power, Heidi made herself the public face of Croissants, personally seating tables, refilling coffee and iced tea, and most importantly, getting to know the guests. Heidi explains, "In a small coastal town like Myrtle Beach, especially back in the 1990s, it was very important to attach a face and a name to a new restaurant to make sure people would feel comfortable enough to come back, and even better, tell their friends about it."

Meanwhile, Heidi was rising at 4 a.m. every day and shuffling her young kids to the restaurant to prepare for the 7 a.m. opening. "They would sleep on the floor while I did the baking and the prep work, and then I would wake them when it was time to go to school," Heidi recalls.

Once she had garnered a local following sufficient to maintain her business, Heidi turned her gaze toward the bakery portion of her operation. "I really wanted the bakery to take off the way breakfast and lunch had," Heidi says. To promote her star culinary players, Heidi offered up the sweet treats to all who entered her café. "I would make our breakfast guests try the cinnamon rolls, and I'd take slices of cake around to every table after they finished lunch," Heidi says. The gestures served to not only highlight the quality of the bakery items at Croissants, but to also cement the impression among diners that Heidi's café was a welcoming place—a Southern place—where guests were treated like family.

SECOND GENERATION

After months of sliding complimentary sweets under her guests' noses to gain their attention, Croissants' bakery sales began to climb. Diners were not only surprised and delighted to be offered a treat to top off their meal, but they were also telling their friends about Croissants' homemade desserts and keeping Heidi in mind when it came time for holidays and special occasions. While Heidi peddled hardest those items close to

gorgeous, custom-made wedding cakes. Stacked high, carefully designed, and individually planned for each bride, Heidi's cakes became the standard for an elegant Myrtle Beach wedding. "Our learning curve was steep in those early years," Heidi recalls. "We were ready to be creative, to make anything the bride could dream up, so some of our creations were happy surprises even to us." Beach themes and flowers were the most common requests, but the Croissants baking team has also been known to create sculpted cakes ranging from golf bags to Corvettes to famous characters.

As the bakery branch of the restaurant developed, more and more locals were enjoying the café and becoming loyal regulars. Art and Carol, whose request for French bread at close of business on that first day was nearly declined, still return to the café weekly—Thursday, to be exact, for the Butternut Squash Soup. They also write a poem for Heidi each year on the anniversary of her opening. Tom and Wrenzie, along with their black lab, Mark, became regular diners on the front patio. "The dog was so big, at first I was afraid he would scare guests away," Heidi says, "but instead he became an icon in the morning. People would ask what was wrong if Mark was not there when they come in for coffee." Another couple, the Hesters, visited Croissants so frequently that other guests would often assume they were the owners. With a daily greeting that often turns into an extended conversation, Heidi has become a part of a routine with each of these guests. The conversations have in turn transformed into friendship over the years, as Heidi enhances the pleasure of the food she serves with warm company to top it off.

her own culinary tradition, like her grandmother's Black Forest Torte, the Southern crowd had their own established opinions. Roz's Carrot Cake and Coconut Custard Cake—with their multiple layers, rich frosting, and decadent textures—reigned supreme among her clientele's tastes, and Heidi had a hard time keeping those items in stock, especially considering their prominent position in the front bakery cases. In those early years, before Heidi expanded her staff, "Holidays were crazy," she recalls. From Christmas through Valentine's Day, Easter, Mother's Day, and Thanksgiving, Heidi and her few employees would be at the bakery until 2 a.m. chopping, baking, and decorating cakes for the morning pickup.

Simultaneously, Myrtle Beach area brides-to-be were discovering Croissants' penchant for creating

THIRD GENERATION

With a strong local following and an equally enthusiastic cadre of seasonal guests, Croissants enjoyed a solid operational foundation throughout the

1990s. Heidi and her café had grown roots in the community, and she was slowly expanding her staff in response to steadily increasing sales in both the café and the bakery portions of the restaurant.

Meanwhile, the Myrtle Beach area had caught the nation's attention. For decades a regional tourist area, it was now attracting visitors from around the country. As the annual number of tourists swelled, national restaurant chains moved to establish a presence in the area. In addition, new shopping centers, shopping malls, and attractions were going up, hoping to gain a piece of the ever-expanding economic pie. New varieties of cuisines, most already familiar to the typical tourist, were popping up all along US 17: Olive Garden, Red Lobster, International House of Pancakes, Carrabba's. The Myrtle Beach restaurant scene began to resemble that of any suburban area along the East Coast. While this competition proved deadly for some local mom-and-pop restaurants, the only effect for Heidi, with her solid local base, was that more seasonal guests began hearing about Croissants.

As restaurants began proliferating in the Myrtle Beach area, so did other types of construction and tourist-driven businesses. Golf courses, office buildings, and condominiums were being planned from Little River to Georgetown, and the newly envisioned Carolina Forest community was starting to take shape. In the midst of this whirlwind of planning and building, a group of local investors approached Heidi about moving the location of her restaurant into a newly developed, more centralized location: the first floor of their building on the corner of 38th Avenue and the recently completed highway, Robert M. Grissom Parkway.

Heidi initially balked at the idea of moving locations when her business was thriving, but by the time the building was completed, she could see the signs of the city evolving and the benefits of moving to the center of the action. She made the leap in 2007, expanding her business from a thirty-five-seat to a seventy-five-seat restaurant. This decision "doubled our square footage and tripled our rent, and we now owed the bank for the upfitting of the new location. Yikes!"

In the first year or two after Croissants' move, Heidi's fears seemed unfounded; business remained strong, and spirits—both hers and those throughout the Myrtle Beach community—were high. "Our business increased significantly after we moved," Heidi recalls. "It was an exciting time." Around the city, property values were up, construction was progressing, the number of annual visitors was soaring, and the potential for the future seemed limitless.

Then, Heidi reports, "The economy tanked."

THE BIG SCRAMBLE

The recession that engulfed the nation did not overlook Myrtle Beach, and every barometer of the tourist industry took a nosedive. Much local construction came to a halt; the housing and real estate markets crumbled; visitors cancelled or shortened their vacations, making a quick jaunt on a shoestring budget; locals dined out rarely, and only at a discounted rate.

Worries about whether she would make rent and payroll each month prompted Heidi to make a significant business decision. Instead of hunkering down and riding out the economic storm, she faced it head on with what could have been a disastrous risk: "I figured, we're paying rent whether we're open or not, so why not open for dinner? So we bought more equipment, expanded the size of the kitchen, added an awning over the outdoor dining area, hired a chef, and voilà! A new endeavor."

However, this was more than an expansion in the hours of Croissants' operation. Instead, it marked a fundamental transformation of the restaurant, its approach to food, and its impact on dining and cuisine in the Myrtle Beach area.

"I am a pastry chef," Heidi explains. I like to cook dinner at home, and I like to eat at fine restaurants, but this was a whole new world for me. I wanted to be in the same category of restaurants where I have had exceptional service and exquisite food. I needed someone to help me bring the bistro to the next culinary level."

IT TAKES A VILLAGE

Heidi's first step in achieving her goal of expanding Croissants' dining repertoire was to find a seasoned chef. Bradley Daniels was in Tennessee when he encountered Heidi's advertisement for an executive chef in the Myrtle Beach area. Though he didn't realize it at the time, his background was a perfect recipe for the kind of culinary leader that would transform the restaurant and fulfill Heidi's vision: a Southern style, a formal education in culinary arts, and a passion for using sustainable practices to create unique dishes from fresh ingredients. Together, over the next four years, Heidi and Brad upped the ante on the Myrtle Beach dining scene and changed the trajectory of Croissants' history. The quaint, quality café emerged as a fine-dining bistro rivaling the menus and ambiance of restaurants in much larger cities.

Though he's a key figure in Croissants' history, Brad is not the only team member to make a significant impact on the restaurant's evolution over the past two decades. Dedicated workers are the lifeblood of the bistro, and Heidi encourages them to write their own chapters in the restaurant's narrative.

Roz Simmons was there the day the Hobart mixer blew up. She comforted Heidi through her panic and doubt, and she appeared bright and early that morning of opening day to create the desserts that would become signature Croissants items. As the café's first baker, she had a huge influence on the development of the bakery menu, and several of her recipes—including Roz's Carrot Cake—are still used today.

Two young sisters, Holly and Courtney Sparks, lived behind Croissants at its original location and came seeking employment when they each turned fifteen. They began assisting in the bakery, baking and decorating cookies, and eventually moved on to other roles in the café. They became such a permanent fixture of the restaurant—with Holly working behind the counter, taking orders, or working in the office and Courtney developing her artistic skills in the cake-decorating department—that people often assumed they were Heidi's children. Guests still ask about them years later, now that they've moved on to new locations and careers.

For years, breakfast patrons knew they would find Walter Jones behind the line each morning, creating their meals to order with a smile on his face. The West Virginia native worked the Croissants breakfast shift for nine years and is remembered perhaps most vividly by Myrtle Beach resident Summer Stewart, who was just a toddler when she would come to Croissants regularly with her grandparents. Each morning, Walter would serve her pancakes custom made into miniature animals.

Other former Croissants employees made such positive and powerful memories at the restaurant that the experience launched their own future careers. Meredith was one of Croissants' very first baristas and worked at the restaurant after graduating from college. Meredith moved to Colorado after working at Croissants, but eventually returned to South Carolina. Spurred by memories of how happy she had been "serving food and making people happy with food," and with her Croissants experience in mind, she opened Three Little Birds Cafe in Folly Beach, South Carolina.

And finally, Heidi's own children all played a role in the development of the restaurant. From washing dishes to managing the dining room to designing advertisements, her personal posse worked from very young ages up through their adulthood to support their mom's business and bring an element of family into the dining room.

It takes a village to operate a restaurant, and Heidi acknowledges and celebrates the team that has contributed not only to Croissants' success but also to its roots and its role in the Myrtle Beach community.

THE NEXT GENERATION . . . AND BEYOND

Over the past several years, Heidi has honed the menu and mission of Croissants to reflect a passion for fine food, a respect for local ingredients, and a bow to the twin traditions of European and Southern cuisine. In doing so, she has created a dining experience that surprises and impresses guests with its whimsy, its variety, and its quality. Croissants' continually evolving seasonal menus are rooted in the land and sea of the Myrtle Beach area, and guests are treated to a fine dining experience within an intimate local setting.

In fact, it's these very guests—Art and Carol, Tom and Wrenzie, the Hesters, and dozens of others— who have prompted this project. "They've been asking for years, 'How come you've never made a cookbook?'" Heidi explains. "Then one day I decided they have a point. It's time to tell my story."

CAROLINA LEMONADE

∿ LIBATIONS ∿

CAROLINA LEMONADE

BANANA CREAM PIE

GARY'S COSMO

WATERMELON FREEZE

THE CHARTIER

CHOCOLATE MARTINI

CUCUMBER MARTINI

SOUTH CAROLINA PEACH AND
BLUEBERRY SANGRIA

———○———

The individual cocktail selection process is—or should be—an intriguing, complex, and sophisticated task. Ideally, one should take into consideration everything from the accompanying food selection, to the time of day, to the company, to the weather. Often we choose cocktails spontaneously, from a gut instinct, but other times a cocktail choice should be carefully planned ahead of time. An outside summer party in the South? Carolina Lemonade. A girls' night out? Chocolate Martini. A romantic dinner? Gary's Cosmo. A beach party? Watermelon Freeze. Many of these drinks were first concocted by Heidi and her husband, Gary, in their home or when entertaining friends, and the most popular ones have made it to the restaurant's menu. Croissants serves these specialty cocktails, in addition to an extensive wine list, to suit every diner's mood, situation, and palate.

Carolina Lemonade

MAKES 1 (4-OUNCE) DRINK

1 shot premium bourbon

1 shot Stirrings Triple Sec

Juice of 1 lemon

1 shot simple syrup

Splash of club soda

1 slice lemon, for garnish

Mix first four ingredients together. Pour over shaved ice in highball glass and top with club soda. Garnish with lemon.

Banana Cream Pie

MAKES 1 (4-OUNCE) DRINK

$1/4$ banana

1 shot Baileys Irish Cream

1 shot Kahlúa

1 shot crème de banana

1 shot vodka

Muddle banana. Add with other ingredients in shaker. Add ice. Shake. Strain.

BANANA CREAM PIE

Gary's Cosmo

MAKES 1 (4-OUNCE) DRINK

1 shot premium vodka

¹/₂ shot Stirrings Triple Sec

¹/₄ shot Cointreau

¹/₄ shot Grand Marnier

1 shot white cranberry juice

1 teaspoon Rose's Lime Juice

2 drops grenadine

1 slice lime, for garnish

Pour all ingredients, except garnish, over ice in shaker. Shake. Strain. Garnish with lime.

Watermelon Freeze

MAKES 4 (8-OUNCE) DRINKS

4 cups watermelon balls scooped from fresh watermelon, deseeded

1 cup vodka

2 tablespoons local, light honey

1 wedge watermelon, for garnish

Freeze watermelon balls overnight. Mix all ingredients, except garnish, in blender until smooth. Pour into four chilled martini glasses. Garnish with watermelon wedge.

CHOCOLATE MARTINI

Chocolate Martini

MAKES 1 (4-OUNCE) DRINK

1 shot Absolut Vodka

1 shot amaretto

1 shot Godiva Milk Chocolate Liqueur

1 Hershey's Milk Chocolate Kiss, frozen

Shaved chocolate, for garnish

Pour all ingredients, except Hershey's Kiss and garnish, over ice in shaker. Shake. Pour into martini glass over Hershey's Kiss. Garnish with shaved chocolate.

The Chartier

FOR THE NONMIXOLOGIST. This drink needs little explanation.

MAKES 1 (4-OUNCE) DRINK

2 shots of your favorite nonspiced dark rum

1 ($2^1/_2$-inch) sphere ice cube

Pour rum over sphere ice cube.

Cucumber Martini

MAKES 1 (4-OUNCE) DRINK

2 slices peeled cucumber

1 shot Hendrick's Gin (or substitute vodka)

$1/2$ shot simple syrup

$1/2$ shot fresh lime juice or Nellie & Joe's Famous Key West Lime Juice

1 slice fresh cucumber, for garnish

1 mint leaf, for garnish

Pour all ingredients, except garnish, over ice in shaker. Shake vigorously. Strain into martini glass. Garnish with cucumber and mint.

South Carolina Peach and Blueberry Sangria

MAKES 25 TO 30 (6-OUNCE) DRINKS

6 ripe peaches

2 (750-milliliter) bottles Riesling or Pinot Grigio

2 (750-milliliter) bottles Chardonnay

1/2 cup peach schnapps

2 quarts blueberries

1 bottle Champagne

Peel and slice peaches and place in beverage server. Add all other ingredients, except Champagne. Let sit for at least a day in the refrigerator. Serve chilled over ice and top each glass with a splash of Champagne.

BREADS

LAVASH

FLATBREAD

FRENCH BREAD

CHALLAH BREAD

RYE BREAD

To many diners, bread is just an afterthought. It's a side item, a vessel to transmit more interesting edibles like sauces and dips, a bookend that holds together the more important ingredients in a sandwich. To foodies and bakers, however, bread is an essential element that can perfect or ruin the quality of a dish. With bland, coarse, or dry bread, everything built upon the foundation falls flat; however, if the bread is appealing in its texture and flavor, it exponentially increases the quality of the meal.

Of course, bread also evokes social communion, playing a key role in bringing people together to share nourishment. Its distinctive aroma is often the catalyst for this phenomenon, as it's difficult not to comment in delight upon entering a kitchen or dining room permeated with the scent of fresh bread. Croissants perpetuates this dynamic, encouraging guests to relax and enjoy themselves by presenting a basket of freshly baked French Bread at every dinner table.

Lavash

LAVASH IS MIDDLE EASTERN in origin and is also known as Armenian cracker bread. A versatile and crunchy dish, Lavash has a wide range of uses as a foundation for spreads or dips, or as a side item with a salad. Variations on the recipe might include a wide range of herbs for enhanced flavor, sesame or caraway seeds sprinkled on top for taste and texture, or different types of pepper incorporated for seasoning. Croissants uses Lavash for its cheese trays. With a side of grapes, olives, or nuts, it makes a lovely appetizer.

MAKES 10 SERVINGS | PREP TIME: 1 HOUR | BAKE TIME: 15 MINUTES

5 cups all-purpose flour

2 teaspoons salt

1 teaspoon sugar

1 $^1/_3$ cup water

2 eggs

3 ounces melted butter, divided

Sea salt and paprika

1. Place flour, salt, and sugar in the bowl of electric mixer fitted with paddle attachment and mix.

2. In a separate bowl whisk together water, eggs, and 2 ounces butter.

3. Gradually add egg mixture to flour mixture. Blend until smooth.

4. Put in bowl that has been buttered, cover with plastic wrap, and allow to rest for about 30 minutes. Meanwhile, preheat oven to 300°F.

5. Roll dough out to $^1/_{16}$-inch thickness and place on the back side of buttered baking sheet. Brush the top with remainder of melted butter. Sprinkle sea salt and paprika on the top.

6. Bake for approximately 10 to 15 minutes, or until golden brown. Cool and break into pieces about 2 by 4 to 6 inches.

Flatbread

FLATBREAD IS A BROAD TERM referring to a range of baked products, some of which are unleavened (made without a leavening agent such as yeast) and possess a crunchy, cracker-type consistency. Croissants makes a leavened flatbread, which is a softer product used for their flatbread pizzas. Flatbread has become exceedingly popular in recent years as a substitute for traditional bread because of its lighter consistency. This flatbread recipe is also convenient, as you can make several loaves and they'll stay fresh in the refrigerator for 4 to 5 days.

MAKES 4 FLATBREADS | PREP TIME: 1 HOUR | BAKE TIME: 10 MINUTES

1 tablespoon active dry yeast

1 1/4 cups warm water (110°F)

3 1/2 cups all-purpose flour

1 tablespoon salt

1 tablespoon sugar

2 tablespoons olive oil, divided

1. Mix yeast into water until dissolved. Set aside.

2. Mix flour, salt, sugar, and 1 tablespoon olive oil in bowl of mixer with dough hook attachment. Add yeast mixture. Knead on low until dough is formed.

3. Separate dough into 4 (6-ounce) portions and roll into balls. Cover with damp towel and let rise for 15 minutes. Meanwhile, preheat oven to 325°F.

4. Roll dough out to about 1/4-inch thickness in preferred shape—round, square, or other. Place on oiled baking sheets. Drizzle the top with remainder of olive oil.

5. Bake for about 10 to 12 minutes.

French Bread

A SIGNATURE CROISSANTS ITEM, French Bread has roots deep in Heidi's family history. Her grandparents in Germany served a small roll—or *brötchen,* German for "small bread"—every morning, with meats and cheeses for adults and Nutella for the grandchildren. In fact, the fresh bread made an appearance on the table at every meal throughout the day. French Bread was a central item when Heidi opened the doors of her bakery and café in 1995, and its aroma permeated the restaurant throughout breakfast and lunch. The recipe continues to hold a focal role on the menu and in the ambiance of the restaurant, as every dinner guest is served complimentary French Bread with sides of sea salt butter and black-eyed pea hummus.

MAKES 6 LOAVES | PREP TIME: 3 HOURS | BAKE TIME: 20 MINUTES

5 tablespoons active, dry yeast

4 cups warm water (110°F)

9 1/2 cups bread flour

2 tablespoons sugar

1 tablespoon salt

1/3 ounce melted butter

Vegetable oil

Cornmeal

1. Mix yeast into water until dissolved. Set aside.

2. In a separate bowl mix flour, sugar, and salt. Add yeast mixture. Then add butter. Knead dough until smooth.

3. Oil sides of large bowl. Place dough in large bowl and cover with clean cloth. Let dough rise for 1 hour.

4. Divide dough into 6 (14-ounce) portions. Roll into French Bread–shaped loaves approximately 22 to 24 inches long.

5. Place loaves on baking pan that has been greased with vegetable oil and sprinkled with cornmeal. Let rise about 1 1/2 hours, or until doubled. Meanwhile, preheat the oven to 400°F.

6. Using a razor or very sharp knife, make 5 to 7 diagonal cuts across the top of the bread.

7. Bake for approximately 20 minutes, spraying with water every 5 minutes to make the crust crispy. Flip loaves during the last 5 minutes of baking to brown the bottoms.

Challah Bread

CHALLAH IS A TRADITIONAL Jewish bread served on the Sabbath and holidays. According to traditional Jewish belief, the bread represents the manna that fell from heaven to feed the people during the Jews' 40-year exile from Egypt. The manna did not fall on the Sabbath or on holidays; instead, a double loaf would fall on the previous day to provide for the Jews on those holy days. Thus today's Challah Bread is braided to represent the abundance of manna on those days. At Croissants, Challah Bread may be found every day of the year, and its buttery, lightly sweet flavor makes spectacular French toast.

MAKES 5 LOAVES | PREP TIME: 5 HOURS | BAKE TIME: 30 MINUTES

5 tablespoons active, dry yeast

2 cups warm water (110°F)

8 egg yolks

4 ounces melted butter

7 1/2 cups bread flour

1/3 cup sugar

1 tablespoon salt

Vegetable oil

2 eggs

1. Mix yeast into water until dissolved. Set aside.

2. In a separate bowl, mix egg yolks, butter, bread flour, sugar, and salt.

3. Add yeast mixture to flour mixture. Knead dough until smooth.

4. Grease a large bowl with vegetable oil. Place dough in bowl and cover with clean cloth. Let rise for about 2 hours, or until doubled in size.

5. Divide into 5 (16-ounce) dough balls. Separate each dough ball into 3 equal pieces.

6. Roll out each piece in a long, thin snake shape. Braid 3 pieces of each loaf to form 5 nice braided loaves.

7. Place loaves on baking pan lined with parchment paper. Let rise for about 1 1/2 hours, or until doubled in size. Meanwhile, preheat the oven to 350°F.

8. Whisk the eggs thoroughly to make an egg wash, then paint the top of each loaf with the egg wash.

9. Bake for approximately 30 minutes, or until golden brown.

Rye Bread

THE DISTINCTIVE FLAVOR of Rye Bread derives largely from the use of rye flour and caraway seeds. Rye flour is denser and darker than other types of flour and also contains less gluten. However, a loaf would not rise properly without the use of other, lighter types of flour. Caraway seeds are a common ingredient in German, Hungarian, and Austrian cuisine, and their nutty flavor plays a key role in the traditional taste of rye bread. Not surprisingly, Croissants uses this homemade Rye Bread for its Reuben sandwich as well as other sandwiches that rotate on the menu.

MAKES 2 LOAVES | PREP TIME: 5 HOURS | BAKE TIME: 30 MINUTES

2 tablespoons active, dry yeast

$2\frac{1}{4}$ cups warm water (110°F), divided

4 tablespoons honey, divided

2 tablespoons caraway seeds

$4\frac{1}{2}$ teaspoons salt

4 cups bread flour, plus more for surface dusting

$2\frac{1}{2}$ cups rye flour

Vegetable oil

1. Combine yeast, $\frac{1}{2}$ cup water, and 1 tablespoon honey. Whisk ingredients together. Let stand about 5 minutes, or until foamy.

2. In the bowl of an electric mixer fitted with a dough hook combine remaining $1\frac{3}{4}$ cups water, 3 tablespoons honey, caraway seeds, salt, and yeast mixture. Mix on low until incorporated. Gradually add both flours, mixing until the dough forms a slightly sticky ball.

3. Grease a large bowl with vegetable oil. Knead dough on floured surface until you can shape it into a ball. Transfer to oiled bowl and cover with plastic wrap.

4. Let dough stand in a warm place about $1\frac{1}{2}$ to 2 hours, until doubled in size.

5. Prepare a sheet pan by lining it with parchment paper and dusting it with flour.

6. Punch down dough and divide in half. Roll each portion into a football shape. Place on prepared sheet pan. Spray a sheet of plastic wrap with nonstick cooking spray and loosely drape over bread loaves.

7. Let rise about 2 more hours, until doubled in size. Meanwhile, preheat oven to 400°F.

8. Remove plastic wrap from bread and use a knife to make 3 diagonal cuts across the top of each loaf.

9. Bake for approximately 30 minutes, or until golden brown.

STARTERS

CRAB CAKES

GRUYÈRE PUFFS

FRENCH ONION SOUP

BUTTERNUT SQUASH SOUP

SHE CRAB SOUP

HEIRLOOM TOMATO SALAD

WATERMELON SALAD

Anticipation: the mood of the starters course. Items on the menu dazzle with their intriguing blend of ingredients, and diners picture the petite portions designed artisanally with creative flourish. A cup of soup, a salad, an indulgent dish of delicate proportion provide diners with an opportunity to try out new flavors and establish the first impression of the dining experience. Starters are fun, and they delight in their own distinct way. Croissants' starters menu rotates, highlighting the flavors of the seasons and manifesting the chef's whimsy according to local availability of ingredients.

At home or a private gathering, starters are the social icebreaker, a way in to conversations and acquaintances that evolve throughout the evening. A few carefully planned appetizers set the mood of the party—elegant or earthy, refined or relaxed. As guests share their initial dining experience, whether the plates are passed or set up buffet style, the tone of the event is established and the road to fun is paved.

Crab Cakes

HANDMADE IS THE OPERATIVE WORD in this recipe. First, working through the lump crabmeat to locate any errant shells is essential. Then, when mixing the crabmeat into the egg mixture and again when forming the cakes, finesse is important; too much mixing will result in the breaking apart of those luscious big chunks of crab. Taking care in the handling of ingredients— much like dealing with the feisty crustacean itself— will lead to the most succulent Crab Cake.

MAKES 6 CAKES | PREP TIME: 15 MINUTES | COOK TIME: 15 MINUTES

1 pound jumbo lump crabmeat

1 tablespoon scallions

2 lemons

2 tablespoons chopped fresh dill

2 tablespoons chopped fresh tarragon

3 egg yolks

1 cup mayonnaise

3 tablespoons stone-ground Dijon mustard

2 teaspoons ground coriander

1 1/2 cups panko bread crumbs

All-purpose flour

Butter

1. Be sure to sift gently through crabmeat and take out any shells. Set aside.

2. Slice scallions on the green end only on a bias. Set aside.

3. Zest and juice lemons. Set juice aside. Mix the zest with dill and tarragon. Set aside.

4. Mix lemon juice, egg yolks, mayonnaise, mustard, and coriander together. Add scallions and dill mixture.

5. Fold in crabmeat, then fold in the panko bread crumbs very gently.

6. Form into approximately 3-ounce cakes and dust in flour.

7. Brown both sides in sauté pan with butter. Finish in oven at 350°F for about 10 minutes, or until heated through.

Gruyère Puffs

SOUTHERN MEETS EUROPEAN yet again, with a blending of traditional tastes. Croissants' recipe combines the pastry of the French *petit choux,* or cream puffs, with soft, tangy cheese to create a dish that rivals the classic Southern cheese straws. Served in the dining room or on the porch swing, these light and cheesy puffs will surprise guests' palates as the delicate exterior of the pastry gives way to the interior richness of Gruyère.

MAKES 2 DOZEN PUFFS | PREP TIME: 1 HOUR | COOK TIME: 30 MINUTES

1 cup water

4 ounces butter, cut into pieces

$^1/_2$ teaspoon salt

1 cup all-purpose flour

4 eggs

$^1/_2$ teaspoon Dijon mustard

1 $^1/_2$ cups grated Gruyère cheese

1. Preheat oven to 450°F.

2. Prepare baking pan by lining with parchment paper.

3. Combine water, butter, and salt in a saucepan over medium heat and bring to a boil. Remove from the heat. Add flour and stir until mixture comes together. Return to low heat and stir for about 5 minutes. Remove from heat and transfer to mixing bowl.

4. Mix with electric mixer on low speed with the paddle until it cools down. Once it has cooled, add 1 egg at a time, mixing in between each addition. Be sure to scrape the sides of the bowl between adding each egg. Once all eggs have been added, mix until creamy. Mix in the mustard and cheese.

5. Scoop with a tablespoon onto prepared baking pan.

6. Bake 5 minutes at 450°F, then turn the oven to 350°F . Cook for about 20 to 25 more minutes, until golden brown.

French Onion Soup

THIS ELEGANT YET HEARTY DISH has taken up permanent residence on Croissants' menu, having headlined the starters list since 1995. The use of homemade French Bread is a refined touch, while the incorporation of Beef Stock, onion, and wine bring a depth of flavor. The melted Gruyère adds a rich and smooth finish.

MAKES 8 SERVINGS | PREP TIME: 25 MINUTES | COOK TIME: 40 MINUTES

10 tablespoons unsalted butter, divided

4 onions, julienned

2 bay leaves

Kosher salt to taste

Black pepper to taste

$1/2$ cup red wine

$1 1/2$ quarts Beef Stock (page 132)

8 thin slices French Bread (page 38)

8 to 16 slices Gruyère cheese

1. Melt 8 tablespoons butter in a large pot over medium heat, moving it around constantly to prevent it from burning. Add the onions and bay leaves, and stir to coat the onions with the melted butter. Season with salt and pepper and continue to stir the onions to allow them to caramelize but prevent them from sticking to the bottom of the pot. Continue to stir the onions until a rich caramel color is formed, about 25 to 30 minutes.

2. Add the red wine, scraping the bottom of the pan to release any onion stuck to the bottom, and bring to a boil. Reduce the heat and simmer until the wine has evaporated and onions are dry.

3. Add the Beef Stock to the pot and simmer for 15 to 20 minutes. While soup is simmering, place French Bread slices under the broiler to toast. Set aside.

4. Season soup with salt and pepper. Remove bay leaves from soup and ladle into crocks. Place French Bread toast on top of the soup. Cover with 1 to 2 slices of Gruyère cheese on each crock. Place under broiler 1 to 2 minutes, until cheese is melted and golden.

Butternut Squash Soup

THURSDAY'S THE DAY for Butternut Squash Soup at Croissants, and plenty of Myrtle Beach locals keep the date open on the calendar. This smooth, rich soup exalts the nutty flavor of the squash and enhances its texture with just a touch of cream cheese. While butternut squash is considered a winter vegetable, it's technically a fruit, and with Croissants' gourmet touch, it remains a favorite all year long.

MAKES 6 SERVINGS | PREP TIME: 30 MINUTES | COOK TIME: 20 MINUTES

3 large butternut squash

Salt and pepper to taste

2 tablespoons olive oil, divided

1 large onion, coarsely diced

1 quart Chicken Stock (page 134)

2 ounces cream cheese

1. Preheat oven to 350°F.

2. Carefully split the squash in half lengthwise. Scoop out the seeds. Season the cut side of the squash with salt and pepper and drizzle with 1 tablespoon of olive oil. Set cut side down on a baking sheet and place in oven for 15 minutes, or until the squash is tender. When cool, scoop out the center using a small spoon.

3. In a large pot over medium-high heat, add remaining olive oil and diced onion. Cook onions until they become translucent, stirring occasionally. Add the roasted squash to the onions along with the Chicken Stock.

4. Bring the stock to a boil, then reduce to a simmer. Simmer on low for 15 minutes. Blend the soup using an immersion blender until smooth. Add the cream cheese and blend again until completely incorporated. Season again with salt and pepper.

She Crab Soup

A TRADITIONAL FAVORITE in the South Carolina lowcountry, She Crab Soup is an elegant and rich bisque-like dish. Original versions of the soup called for crab roe in addition to lump crabmeat, so females were separated from the catch to be destined for the soup pot. While most modern recipes use solely crabmeat without the roe, the female moniker remains.

MAKES 8 TO 10 SERVINGS | PREP AND COOK TIME: 30 MINUTES

$1/4$ pound butter

$1/4$ cup flour

2 cups small diced celery

2 cups diced onion

$1/2$ cup sherry

2 quarts heavy cream

$1/2$ teaspoon nutmeg

1 pound jumbo lump crabmeat

Salt and pepper to taste

---

1. In a large pot over high heat, melt butter and add flour, mixing well. Cook until a blonde roux is formed. Reduce heat to medium. Add the celery and onions and cook until onions are translucent. Deglaze the pot with sherry. Move to double boiler.

2. Add heavy cream. Bring to a boil. Add nutmeg.

3. Gently fold in crabmeat.

4. Thin with additional cream if necessary. Season with salt and pepper.

Heirloom Tomato Salad

THIS SALAD HAILS SUMMER, when Diane at the farmer's market on 79th Avenue in Myrtle Beach is peddling her freshest South Carolina tomatoes of the season. Pair them with cheese made from goat's milk at Worley Lane Farms, fresh basil from the herb garden, and slices of fresh Challah Bread, and you've got more than a salad; you've got a hearty sandwich/salad combo that becomes a lasting memory.

MAKES 4 SERVINGS | PREP TIME: 10 MINUTES

8 slices Challah Bread (page 40)

12 ounces goat cheese

Butter

12 heirloom tomato slices

Salt and pepper to taste

12 leaves fresh basil, chopped

4 basil leaves, for garnish

Olive oil

Balsamic Reduction (page 131)

1. Spread 4 slices of Challah Bread with 3 ounces of goat cheese each and use the remaining slices to make 4 sandwiches. Spread the outsides of the sandwiches with butter.

2. Grill both sides until golden brown.

3. Place each sandwich on a plate. Top each sandwich with a slice of tomato, then sprinkle with salt, pepper, and fresh basil. Repeat 2 more times. Top with 1 basil leaf. Drizzle with olive oil and Balsamic Reduction.

Watermelon Salad

THIS DISH COMBINES the best of fresh summer produce with a touch of Mediterranean flair to produce a light and refreshing salad that hits Croissants' menu in early summer each year. It's Greek meets Southern, and the results are so good that diners don't know whether to pair it with ouzo or sweet tea.

MAKES 4 SERVINGS | PREP TIME: 10 MINUTES

4 thick slices of seedless watermelon

16 cucumber slices

1 yellow tomato, quartered

1 slice finely shaved onion

1/8 cup Kalamata olive slices

1/8 cup toasted pine nuts

Olive oil

Salt and pepper to taste

1 cup Tzatziki Dressing (page 141)

Balsamic Reduction (page 131)

4 mint leaves, for garnish

1. Toss watermelon, cucumber, tomato, onion, olive slices, and pine nuts in bowl with a little olive oil, salt, and pepper.

2. Pour 1/4 cup Tzatziki Dressing in the center of each plate. Place watermelon slice on top. Stack cucumbers on top of the watermelon. Place 1/4 tomato next to cucumber stack. Place onions, olive slices, and pine nuts on top.

3. Drizzle with Balsamic Reduction. Top with mint leaf.

THE MAIN

SHRIMP AND GRITS

SCALLOPS BENTON

PAN-SEARED GROUPER

ANGRY BULLS BAY CLAMS

BISTRO CHICKEN

PEACH PORK TENDERLOIN

———————◦———————

For Croissants, the essence of a seasonal menu is its fluidity. When it comes to creating entrées—the centerpiece of the Southern dining experience—the chef develops a vision of the final concept and remains open to the daily possibilities of specific ingredients. From there, it's all about the reports coming in from farmers and fishermen around the Myrtle Beach area. "When I call Cindy from Worley Lane Farms and she tells me the goats are making milk, then we'll put goat cheese on the menu," Heidi says. "When the fish are biting, I call Wayne at Kenyon Seafood in Murrells Inlet to see what he's got. Whether it's grouper or snapper or hogfish, his daily catch winds up on our plates that evening." Some purveyors are able to provide a local product that becomes an annual staple, such as clams from Bulls Bay or tomatoes from Diane at the farmer's market on 79th Avenue. The plates are constructed piecemeal, each element handpicked from the native bounty to create fresh tastes unique to the area.

Shrimp and Grits

"AN INEXPENSIVE, SIMPLE, and thoroughly digestible food, [grits] should be made popular throughout the world. Given enough of it, the inhabitants of planet Earth would have nothing to fight about. A man full of [grits] is a man of peace." So declared the South Carolina General Assembly, designating grits the official state food in 2000.

Croissants' version of the classic Southern dish may vary with the seasons, but its foundation is consistent: Adluh grits, produced by Adluh Flour Mills in Columbia, South Carolina, since 1900, are the only grits that grace the plate in Croissants' dining room.

MAKES 4 SERVINGS | PREP TIME: 45 MINUTES | COOK TIME: 30 MINUTES

FOR THE SHRIMP:

1 tablespoon olive oil

1 cup diced yellow onion

1 tablespoon finely chopped garlic

$2/3$ cup diced red bell pepper

4 ounces andouille sausage, cooked and cut in $1/2$-inch cubes

24 large shrimp

1 cup white wine

1 tablespoon chopped parsley

Red pepper flakes

$1/2$ cup heavy cream

Salt and pepper to taste

FOR THE FRIED GREEN TOMATOES:

$1 1/2$ cups all-purpose flour

$1 1/2$ cups finely stone-ground cornmeal

$1 1/2$ teaspoons paprika

$1 1/2$ teaspoons garlic powder

$1 1/2$ teaspoons black pepper

3 teaspoons kosher salt

3 cups buttermilk

Salt and pepper to taste

3 green tomatoes, ends removed, thickly sliced into 4 slices each

$3/4$ cup vegetable oil

FOR THE ASSEMBLY:

2 cups Pimento Cheese Grits (page 136)

$1/4$ cup chopped scallions, for garnish

FOR THE SHRIMP:

1. Heat olive oil in a large sauté pan over medium heat. Add onion, garlic, and red bell pepper. Cook until they begin to caramelize.

2. Add sausage and shrimp. Cook until shrimp are pink, about 3 minutes depending on the size. Remove the shrimp from the pan and set aside for final assembly.

3. Add white wine, parsley, and pepper flakes to taste and cook about 5 minutes to reduce a bit.

4. Add heavy cream and remove from heat. Salt and pepper to taste.

FOR THE FRIED GREEN TOMATOES:

1. In a large bowl, combine the flour, cornmeal, and spices. Pour the buttermilk into a separate bowl and season with salt and pepper. Place the tomatoes in the buttermilk, then lightly dredge them in the flour mixture, thoroughly coating both sides.

2. Using a large cast-iron skillet on medium-high heat, cover the bottom with the oil. When the oil is hot (350°F), carefully lay the tomato slices in the oil, panfrying them until they are golden brown on each side, about 3 to 4 minutes. This may need to be done in batches to prevent the oil from cooling.

3. Remove the crispy golden brown tomatoes and drain on paper towels.

FOR THE ASSEMBLY:

Ladle andouille sausage mixture into each bowl. Place 1/2 cup Grits down the center. Lay 3 fried green tomato slices on the Grits and top each with 2 interlocking large shrimp. Garnish with scallions.

Scallops Benton

SUCCULENT SCALLOPS MAY BE the star of the dish, but the supporting roles of fresh Southern corn and smoky bacon deserve accolades as well. This recipe rotates onto the menu in late May each year, when local corn makes its debut on area farms, and closes its run in late September. The sweet flavor of the corn permeates the puree as well as adding a complementary pop to the tenderness of the shellfish. Meanwhile, the salty cured meat, which hails solely from Benton's Smoky Mountain Country Hams in Madisonville, Tennessee, adds heartiness and texture to the dish.

MAKES 4 SERVINGS | PREP TIME: 20 MINUTES | COOK TIME: 25 MINUTES

FOR THE PUREE:

1 tablespoon extra-virgin olive oil

1 tablespoon shaved garlic

1 tablespoon shaved shallots

1 tablespoon chopped thyme

2 cups corn, cut from cob

1 cup heavy cream

FOR THE CORN:

2 tablespoons extra-virgin olive oil

2 tablespoons shaved garlic

2 tablespoons shaved shallots

2 cups corn, cut from cob

1 cup grape tomatoes, split lengthwise

2 tablespoons torn basil

Salt and pepper to taste

2 tablespoons butter

FOR THE BACON AND SCALLOPS:

4 slices thick-cut Benton's bacon

24 ounces scallops

Salt and pepper to taste

FOR THE PUREE:

1. Heat the olive oil in a sauté pan over medium-high heat; add garlic, shallots, and thyme. Stir the garlic mixture and add corn. Sauté for 3 minutes, stirring occasionally.

2. Add cream and bring to a boil. Allow to boil for 30 seconds.

3. Pour contents into a blender. (Note: Take caution in blending hot liquids in a blender.) Pulse the blender to start before pureeing completely, as hot liquids will expand.

FOR THE CORN:

1. Heat the olive oil in a sauté pan over medium-high heat. Add garlic and toast it until golden brown, being careful not to burn it.

2. Add shallots, corn, and tomatoes and cook until tender.

3. Add basil, salt, pepper, and butter to finish.

FOR THE BACON AND SCALLOPS:

1. Cook the bacon by placing in a large sauté pan on medium heat. Allow the bacon to cook and begin to crisp. Flip and cook on the other side.

2. Remove the bacon and place on a paper towel to absorb excess grease. Using the same pan, season scallops with salt and pepper and carefully place in bacon drippings. Allow the scallops to cook on first side until they begin to caramelize, about 2 to 3 minutes. Flip scallops and repeat on other side.

FOR THE ASSEMBLY:

Place a large spoonful of the puree on the bottom of the plate. Lay bacon on top of the puree and the scallops on top of the bacon. Place a large spoonful of the sautéed corn beside the scallops.

Pan-Seared Grouper

THIS RECIPE STARTS WITH fresh local fish caught from the waters off Murrells Inlet, South Carolina. Wayne Mershon, owner of Kenyon Seafood, takes his boats daily through the marsh and into the Atlantic's Gulf Stream to seek the catch that ultimately lands in Croissants' kitchen.

The chef lays the foundation of this dish with tastes of summer: creamy red potatoes for texture and fresh corn for a burst of color. The hearty grouper filets, after a quick sear to seal in flavor, are topped with an authentically Southern concoction of smoky bacon and sweet, ripe tomatoes.

MAKES 4 SERVINGS | PREP TIME: 30 MINUTES | COOK TIME: 30 MINUTES

FOR THE POTATOES:

6 red bliss potatoes, quartered

1 tablespoon olive oil

Salt and pepper to taste

FOR THE GROUPER:

1 tablespoon olive oil

4 (7- to 8-ounce) skin-on grouper filets, each 1- to 1¼-inches thick

Salt and pepper to taste

FOR THE VEGETABLES:

2 tablespoons butter, divided

1 red onion, julienned

1 cup yellow corn, cut from cob

6 grape tomatoes or 1 large tomato, diced

1½ cups fresh spinach

Salt and pepper to taste

FOR THE ASSEMBLY:

4 tablespoons Bacon and Tomato Jam (page 130)

FOR THE POTATOES:

1. Preheat oven to 350°F.

2. In a large bowl, toss the potatoes with olive oil, salt, and pepper.

3. Lay the potatoes on a sheet pan and roast in the oven for 15 minutes, or until golden brown.

FOR THE GROUPER:

1. Heat olive oil in a medium-size pan on medium-high heat.

2. Season the filets with salt and pepper, and place skin side down in the pan.

3. Lightly press down on the fish with a spatula to ensure that the skin gets crispy.

4. Cook the fish about 3 minutes on each side, or until golden brown.

FOR THE VEGETABLES:

1. In a second medium-size pan on medium-high heat, melt 1 tablespoon of butter.

2. Add the onion and cook for 1 minute. Add corn and the prepared roasted potatoes and cook for 3 minutes.

3. Complete the vegetables by adding tomatoes and spinach. Season with salt and pepper.

FOR THE ASSEMBLY:

Place a large spoonful of the sautéed vegetables in the center of a plate. Top the vegetables with the grouper, adding a tablespoon of the Bacon and Tomato Jam on top.

Angry Bulls Bay Clams

JUST NORTH OF CHARLESTON, South Carolina, lies Bulls Bay, an inlet of the Atlantic Ocean brimming with saltwater shellfish. Bill Livingston, of Livingston's Bulls Bay Seafood in McClellanville, has been harvesting those treasures since 1995, even running his boats twenty-four hours a day during the spring. This recipe, created by chef Bradley Daniels, has been a staple on Croissants' menu since 2010, and the Livingston's "clam man" receives a warm reception as he arrives with the tender, salty gems.

MAKES 4 SERVINGS | PREP TIME: 20 MINUTES | COOK TIME: 25 MINUTES

4 pounds Bulls Bay clams (or any fresh clams)

1 teaspoon olive oil

2 tablespoons sliced garlic cloves

2 tablespoons roughly chopped cherry bomb peppers

2 tablespoons sliced shallots

1 1/2 cups white wine

4 tablespoons butter

1/2 cup cherry tomatoes, cut lengthwise

6 large basil leaves, torn

1 1/2 cups favorite pasta, cooked

Salt, pepper, and red pepper flakes to taste

1. Clean the clams by rinsing them under cold water to remove sand.

2. Using a large sauté pan or pot with a lid, heat oil and garlic over medium heat. Stir lightly until garlic is toasted, being careful not to burn it. Add the peppers, shallots, and clams.

3. Stir the mixture and add wine and butter. Bring the wine and butter to a boil, cover, and cook until the clams open.

4. Remove the lid and add tomatoes, basil, and cooked pasta. Season with salt and pepper. Use the red pepper flakes to adjust the "angry" to your taste. Discard any unopened shells.

5. Divide pasta into serving bowls and top with clams.

Bistro Chicken

THIS CLASSIC DISH, heralding Heidi's European roots, has held a central role on the Croissants menu since the bistro's early days. Through minor variations, the flavors on the plate have remained consistent for nearly a decade. The tangy Gournay Cheese and sun-dried tomatoes blend seamlessly with fresh basil, while prosciutto adds heartiness to the chicken. The mushrooms and spinach bring unexpected texture and dimension to the pasta, resulting in a dish with stellar visual appeal. Though any form of pasta will fit the recipe, Croissants uses homemade fettuccini pasta cut wide.

MAKES 4 SERVINGS | PREP TIME: 90 MINUTES | COOK TIME: 35 MINUTES

FOR THE CHICKEN:

4 chicken breasts

4 ounces prosciutto, thinly sliced

4 ounces softened Gournay Cheese (page 133), divided

$^1/_8$ cup basil

$^1/_2$ cup diced sun-dried tomatoes

2 eggs, beaten

$^1/_2$ cup milk

$^1/_4$ cup flour

1 cup panko bread crumbs

1 tablespoon butter

FOR THE PASTA:

1 tablespoon olive oil

2 teaspoons shaved garlic

2 teaspoons shaved shallots

1 cup sliced mushrooms

1 cup baby spinach

2 cups Classico Sauce (page 135)

FOR THE ASSEMBLY:

2 cups favorite pasta, cooked

2 tablespoons Balsamic Reduction (page 131)

Salt and pepper to taste

FOR THE CHICKEN:

1. Preheat oven to 350°F.

2. Cut a slit in each chicken breast lengthwise to make a pocket.

3. Spread 1 ounce of Gournay Cheese on prosciutto. Lay inside chicken pockets. Lay basil and sun-dried tomatoes on top of the Gournay Cheese inside the chicken breast. Spread remaining Gournay Cheese along the edge of pockets and pinch to seal.

4. Create egg wash by whisking eggs with milk in small bowl.

5. Dredge chicken breasts in flour, then dip in egg wash. While wet, dip in panko bread crumbs to cover both sides.

6. Melt butter over medium heat in sauté pan. Add chicken to brown both sides.

7. Bake chicken breasts for about 10 to 20 minutes (depending on their size) to finish. Remove from the oven and allow to rest for 5 minutes.

FOR THE PASTA:

1. Heat olive oil and garlic in a large sauté pan over medium-high heat. Allow the garlic to begin to slightly brown, then add the shallots and mushrooms.

2. Sauté the garlic, shallot, and mushroom mixture for about 3 minutes.

3. Add the spinach and stir. Cook for another 3 minutes.

4. Add the Classico Sauce to vegetable mixture and cook for 2 minutes.

FOR THE ASSEMBLY:

1. Divide pasta into bowls.

2. Pour the vegetable and tomato sauce over pasta.

3. Cut the chicken breasts in half and lay on top of the pasta. Drizzle with Balsamic Reduction.

4. Season with salt and pepper.

Peach Pork Tenderloin

TO CELEBRATE THE POPULARITY of one of its top agricultural products, South Carolina holds an annual Peach Day in Columbia each June. If you miss the event, though, this dish—which hails summertime in the South—might hold you over till next year. The sweet, fresh fruit is lightly charred on the grill, lending it depth to balance the pungency of the onion. Both flavors complement the juicy pork, while the sweet acidity of the barbeque sauce is just rich enough to perfectly finish the dish.

MAKES 4 SERVINGS | PREP TIME: 90 MINUTES | COOK TIME: 30 MINUTES

FOR THE PORK:

2 (1-pound) pork tenderloins

1 tablespoon olive oil

Salt and pepper to taste

1 cup Peach BBQ Sauce (page 140)

FOR THE POTATOES:

1 ¹/₂ pounds red bliss potatoes, quartered

1 tablespoon olive oil

Salt and pepper to taste

FOR THE PEACHES AND VEGETABLES:

4 fresh peaches, sliced

1 red onion, julienned

1 tablespoon olive oil

Salt and pepper to taste

1 cup baby spinach

FOR THE ASSEMBLY:

¹/₂ cup Peach BBQ Sauce

FOR THE PORK:

1. Preheat the grill to medium-high heat.

2. Rub the pork tenderloins with the olive oil and season with salt and pepper generously.

3. Place the tenderloins on the grill grate and allow to cook 3 to 5 minutes per side. Keep rotating the pork to ensure that it is cooking evenly. Brush each tenderloin with ¹/₂ cup of the Peach BBQ Sauce. Cook until the internal temperature reaches 155°F. Remove from the grill and allow to rest for 5 to 10 minutes before slicing.

FOR THE POTATOES:

1. Preheat the oven to 350°F.

2. Toss the quartered potato wedges with the olive oil in a large bowl. Season with salt and pepper and place on a baking sheet.

3. Place the sheet in the oven and bake for 10 to 15 minutes, or until the potatoes are golden brown.

FOR THE PEACHES AND VEGETABLES:

1. In a large bowl, add the cooked potatoes, sliced peaches, and onion. Toss with the olive oil and season with salt and pepper. Pour the whole vegetable mix over the grill grate. Spread the mixture out in an even layer to ensure that all pieces are cooked evenly.

2. Allow to cook for 4 to 5 minutes, then turn over on the grill. Continue cooking until the vegetables and the peaches are cooked.

3. Transfer the ingredients back to a bowl and add the spinach. Toss all the ingredients together and reseason with salt and pepper.

FOR THE ASSEMBLY:

Put 2 tablespoons of Peach BBQ Sauce on each plate and spoon the vegetables over the sauce. Slice the well-rested tenderloins and shingle over the mixture.

BRUNCH

SMOTHERED GRITS

GRANOLA

BANANAS FOSTER FRENCH TOAST

CROQUE MONSIEUR /
CROQUE MADAME

STRAWBERRY CREPES / BANANA
AND NUTELLA CREPES

ARTICHOKE AND PIMENTO
CHEESE SANDWICH

HAM, APPLE, AND BRIE MELT

MONTE CRISTO

CAPRESE FLATBREAD

FRESH PEACH AND
PROSCIUTTO FLATBREAD

Ahhh, brunch—that lovely time of the week that's as much a mind-set as a meal. Rising late, leisurely drinking a cup of coffee and reading the newspaper, and finally getting around to a luxurious and beautiful plate of food that spans two meals: that defines the ultimate weekend morning for those who indulge in brunch.

When Croissants opened in 1995, brunch was a rare find in Myrtle Beach. Breakfast restaurants were largely limited to pancake houses or mom-and-pop establishments serving eggs and bacon with a side of grits. Sunday breakfast might include an all-you-can-eat buffet to be enjoyed after church at some of the more traditional restaurants, but no one was serving the unique breakfast/lunch combination that begs to be paired with a Bloody Mary or mimosa.

Heidi began serving weekend brunch at Croissants in 2011, and the environment as well as the menu (not to mention the build-your-own Bloody Mary bar) provides a perfect and classic brunch experience. Some recipes are sweet, some savory, some fun, but all provide a nice range of choices to suit the tastes of the breakfast crowd, the lunch crowd, and those who fit somewhere in between.

Smothered Grits

THIS RECIPE TAKES PERHAPS the most definitive Southern dish and puts a fresh local twist on it. The Grits are combined with farm-fresh produce (a much tastier and healthier variation than the traditional butter and salt). Add fried or poached eggs and top with Ham Hock Jus, and you've got a hearty and beautiful brunch dish that maintains its Southern roots while appealing to modern tastes. Croissants added the dish to the menu when it began serving brunch in 2011, and it's been a crowd-pleaser ever since.

MAKES 1 SERVING | PREP TIME: 45 MINUTES | COOK TIME: 10 MINUTES

1 tablespoon vegetable oil

1 cup diced country ham

1/2 cup grape tomatoes, halved

1/2 cup fresh corn cut from the cob

2 tablespoons diced onion

1 cup creamy or savory Grits (page 136)

2 eggs, prepared the way you like them

2 tablespoons Ham Hock Jus (page 137)

1. Heat vegetable oil in a sauté pan over medium heat.

2. Sauté ham, tomatoes, corn, and onion until warm. Set aside.

3. Place Grits in the center of a bowl. Spoon ham and vegetable mixture around Grits.

4. Place two eggs (scrambled, poached, or fried) on top. Drizzle with Ham Hock Jus.

Granola

SOMETIMES, CRUNCHY AND EARTHY is the craving of the day. This fresh granola is a nutty, hearty mixture baked to perfection, and it's full of protein for long-lasting energy. Served with fresh berries and yogurt, this complex blend of flavors brings the term *cereal* to a whole new level. Made at home, it's a great on-the-go breakfast or snack.

MAKES 8 TO 10 SERVINGS | PREP TIME: 5 MINUTES | BAKE TIME: 15 MINUTES

9 tablespoons vegetable oil, divided

4 cups oats

2 1/2 cups sliced almonds

1 1/2 cups coconut flakes

1/2 teaspoon salt

1/2 cup honey

1 cup dried cranberries

1 cup golden raisins

1. Preheat oven to 375°F.

2. Prepare baking sheet by coating with 1 tablespoon vegetable oil.

3. Toss together oats, almonds, coconut, and salt.

4. Whisk together 8 tablespoons oil and honey. Stir into oat mixture.

5. Spread mixture on baking sheet.

6. Bake for 15 minutes, mixing occasionally.

7. Remove from oven and mix in cranberries and raisins.

Bananas Foster French Toast

EVER SINCE IT WAS first served at Brennan's restaurant in New Orleans with a dramatic flambé preparation, bananas Foster has been synonymous with sweet indulgence. This brunch recipe preserves the classic caramelized flavors and the *brûlée* (French for "burnt") technique of the dessert. The adaptation of the dessert into a topping for French toast, combined with the use of the buttery Challah Bread, makes this a unique and popular item on Croissants' brunch menu.

MAKES 4 SERVINGS | PREP TIME: 15 MINUTES | COOK TIME: 5 MINUTES

FOR THE SYRUP:

8 ounces butter

2 cups brown sugar

3 ounces dark spiced rum

1 cup heavy cream

FOR THE BANANAS:

Granulated sugar

2 bananas, sliced in half lengthwise

FOR THE TOAST:

3 eggs

1 cup milk

1 teaspoon vanilla

1 teaspoon cinnamon

8 slices Challah Bread page 40)

1 tablespoon butter

FOR THE ASSEMBLY:

Real whipped cream or powdered sugar

FOR THE SYRUP:

1. Melt butter in saucepan. Add brown sugar. Stir until combined.

2. Add spiced rum.

3. Reduce for 5 minutes.

4. Add heavy cream. Mix well. Set aside.

FOR THE BANANAS:

1. Sprinkle sugar on top of each banana on the side that has been cut.

2. Brûlée the tops with a torch or under broiler until golden brown. Set aside.

FOR THE TOAST:

1. Beat eggs. Add milk, vanilla, and cinnamon.

2. Dip each slice of bread in milk mixture and turn over to coat both sides.

3. Place in heated sauté pan with melted butter. Cook until golden brown.

4. Turn and cook the other side until golden brown. You may need to add a little more butter during cooking.

FOR THE ASSEMBLY:

1. Place 2 slices of French toast on each plate. Top with brûléed banana.

2. Drizzle with syrup and top with real whipped cream or powdered sugar.

Croque Monsieur / Croque Madame

THIS GRILLED HAM AND CHEESE sandwich has deep roots in French culture; its first appearance on a menu was recorded in a Parisian café in 1910, and Marcel Proust makes mention of the snack in his most famous work, *In Search of Lost Time.* With its name deriving from the French verb *croquer* (to crunch) and the term monsieur (mister), this dish is still quite common in French bars and cafés. Croissants' version uses Challah Bread, which is the perfect consistency to stand up to grilling, and adds cheese to the béchamel, resulting in a Mornay Sauce. Similar to the Croque Monsieur in both its ingredients and its history, the Croque Madame is topped with 2 eggs (hence the feminine title), resulting in an even richer and more satisfying dish.

MAKES 1 SANDWICH | PREP TIME: 10 MINUTES | COOK TIME: 5 MINUTES

FOR CROQUE MONSIEUR:

1 slice Challah Bread (page 40)

1 egg

Water

Butter

6 ounces thinly sliced ham

2 slices Gruyère cheese

2 tablespoons Mornay Sauce (page 138)

FOR CROQUE MADAME:

1 Croque Monsieur (left)

2 eggs

Butter

1 tablespoon Mornay Sauce

FOR CROQUE MONSIEUR:

1. Set oven to broil. Prepare baking sheet by covering with parchment paper.

2. Dip bread in egg wash made of 1 part egg and 1 part water. Place in sauté pan with a little melted butter. Cook both sides.

3. Stack ham on top of bread and top with slices of Gruyère.

4. Place under broiler until cheese is brown, then drizzle with Mornay Sauce.

FOR CROQUE MADAME:

1. Prepare Croque Monsieur.

2. Fry 2 eggs in sauté pan with a little melted butter. Cook to preferred preparation: over easy, sunny-side up, etc.

3. Place eggs on top of Croquet Monsieur and top with Mornay Sauce.

Strawberry Crepes / Banana and Nutella Crepes

AS A CHILD, HEIDI REMEMBERS her grand-mother making *pfannkuchen* (German for "pan-cake"), and the little girl thought it was strange that they were so skinny. The thin pastry is of course a French crepe, and as Heidi came to realize, this dish is more about what's inside than the pancake holding it together. Sweet or savory, crepes take on any flavor and make it a bit more sophisticated. Croissants serves several variations on this classic French dish, and the ones we've included here are both a big hit with children.

MAKES 8 CREPES | PREP TIME: 20 MINUTES | COOK TIME: 2 MINUTES EACH

FOR THE CREPES:

2 eggs

1 cup milk

1 cup all-purpose flour

1 tablespoon melted butter

Pinch nutmeg

Pinch kosher salt

1 teaspoon vegetable oil

FOR STRAWBERRY CREPES:

3 cups fresh strawberries, divided

1 teaspoon granulated sugar

8 tablespoons plain yogurt

Powdered sugar

FOR BANANA AND NUTELLA CREPES:

1 cup Nutella

8 bananas

Powdered sugar or real whipped cream

FOR THE CREPES:

1. Add all ingredients, except vegetable oil, into a blender and blend until smooth.

2. Heat a 9-inch skillet over medium heat. Pour vegetable oil in a nonstick pan. Continue to heat until bubbling.

3. Pour 2 ounces of crepe batter into pan. Tilt pan to cover the bottom.

4. Cook until golden. Turn crepe over in pan and cook the other side until golden. Repeat steps 3 and 4 to make 7 more crepes.

FOR STRAWBERRY CREPES:

1. Cut 1 1/2 cups strawberries into small pieces. Place them in a bowl and top with granulated sugar to macerate. Set aside until the sugar becomes like a syrup.

2. Spread 1 tablespoon yogurt on each crepe. Cut the remaining strawberries and lay them all over crepe. Roll up like a cigar.

3. Top with macerated strawberries and powdered sugar.

FOR BANANA AND NUTELLA CREPES:

1. Spread 2 tablespoons Nutella on each crepe. Lay whole banana on crepe.

2. Begin at one side and roll crepe like a cigar.

3. Top with powdered sugar or real whipped cream

Artichoke and Pimento Cheese Sandwich

SOUTHERNERS DO LOVE their pimento cheese; it's a staple everywhere from picnics to cocktail parties across the region, and it's proudly served on white bread for only $1.50 at the venerable Masters Tournament each spring in Augusta, Georgia. Croissants' manifestation of the "pate of the South" takes the form of an open-faced sandwich, and its flavor, blended with artichokes and smoked turkey, has become a standing favorite among locals and visitors alike.

MAKES 1 SANDWICH | PREP TIME: 10 MINUTES | COOK TIME: 10 MINUTES

2 artichoke hearts, cut in half

1 slice Rye Bread (page 41, or you can substitute any bread)

1 leaf lettuce

2 slices tomato

4 ounces smoked turkey

1 to 2 tablespoons Pimento Cheese (page 139)

1. Grill or sauté artichoke hearts. Set aside.

2. Set oven to broil. Prepare baking sheet by covering with parchment paper.

3. Place slice of bread on baking sheet. Layer with lettuce, tomato, and smoked turkey. Top with Pimento Cheese.

4. Place in oven under broiler about 3 minutes, or until Pimento Cheese is melted.

5. Remove from oven and top with artichoke hearts.

Ham, Apple, and Brie Melt

THIS PARTICULAR COMBINATION of flavors is a Croissants original. Deconstructed, this sandwich's ingredients resemble a cheeseboard; unified in a sandwich, each item is showcased in layers of color, texture, and taste: the saltiness of the ham, the sweet tanginess of the apple, and the creamy richness of the Brie. Stacked on a buttery, flaky croissant, this sandwich makes for a hearty, unique, and delicious lunch.

MAKES 1 SANDWICH | PREP TIME: 10 MINUTES | COOK TIME: 5 MINUTES

1 large croissant

1 tablespoon honey mustard

4 to 8 ounces of thinly sliced ham

4 slices of green or red apples, about $\frac{1}{4}$ inch thick

1 ($\frac{1}{4}$-inch) slice Brie cheese

1. Set oven to broil. Prepare baking sheet by covering with parchment paper.

2. Cut croissant in half lengthwise and spread one half with honey mustard.

3. Place ham on bread, followed by the apples and Brie, then place on prepared pan.

4. Place in oven under the broiler until cheese is melted, and voilà!

Monte Cristo

THIS CLASSIC FRENCH SANDWICH is a variation on the Croque Monsieur, equally popular and legendary in French culture. The bread is grilled in a traditional French toast style, resulting in a sophisticated deli-type sandwich. Rather than being covered in Mornay Sauce, this item is served with a tangy lingonberry or cranberry sauce, making it easier to pick up and enjoy.

MAKES 1 SANDWICH | PREP TIME: 10 MINUTES | COOK TIME: 10 MINUTES

1 tablespoon butter

1 egg

¼ cup milk

2 slices Challah Bread (page 40)

4 ounces ham

4 ounces roasted or smoked turkey

2 slices Swiss cheese

2 ounces lingonberry sauce or cranberry sauce

1. Melt butter in a sauté pan over medium heat.

2. Beat egg and add milk. Dip each slice of bread in milk mixture and cook one side of each slice in sauté pan. Turn each slice of bread.

3. Stack ham, turkey, and cheese on one slice of bread. Cover with the second slice of bread with the cooked side facing in.

4. Cook each side until golden brown. You may want to cover pan while cooking each side in order to heat the meat and melt the cheese. Serve with lingonberry or cranberry sauce.

Caprese Flatbread

THE TERM *CAPRESE* often refers to a salad of basil, tomato, and mozzarella, which is commonly understood to represent the red, green, and white colors in the Italian flag. Manifested as a pizza, these three classic ingredients blend deliciously, especially when each is fresh and seasonal.

MAKES 1 FLATBREAD PIZZA | PREP TIME: 10 MINUTES | BAKE TIME: 8 MINUTES

1 Flatbread (page 37)

1/4 cup Classico Sauce (page 135)

1 fresh tomato, sliced

4 ounces grated fresh mozzarella

1 cup chopped fresh basil

1. Preheat oven to 350°F. Prepare baking pan by coating with nonstick spray.

2. Top flatbread with sauce, tomato, mozzarella, and basil, in that order.

3. Bake about 8 minutes, or until cheese is melted.

Fresh Peach and Prosciutto Flatbread

PEACH ON A PIZZA may seem strange to some, but for South Carolinians, the honorable fruit may go where none other has gone before. That's because, according to the *Charleston Post and Courier,* South Carolina is the largest peach-producing state on the East Coast, annually growing three times as many as Georgia. So peaches on a pizza is a perfectly reasonable—and delicious—notion, especially when their sweet taste is combined with the saltiness of prosciutto and crunch of fresh arugula.

MAKES 1 FLATBREAD PIZZA | PREP TIME: 15 MINUTES

1 Flatbread (page 37)

1 cup arugula

1 peach, sliced

1 tablespoon olive oil

2 to 4 slices prosciutto, thinly sliced

2 ounces shaved Parmesan cheese

1 tablespoon Balsamic Reduction (page 131)

Salt and pepper to taste

1. Preheat oven to 350°F.

2. Reheat flatbread in oven for about 5 minutes.

3. Mix arugula and peach slices in bowl with olive oil. Place on top of warm flatbread.

4. Lay prosciutto on top of arugula, followed by Parmesan cheese.

5. Drizzle with Balsamic Reduction. Season with salt and pepper.

COCONUT MACAROONS

COOKIES

ROZ'S CHOCOLATE
CHIP COOKIES

GRANDMA ERB'S
MOLASSES COOKIES

CROISSANTS' SIGNATURE
BROWNIES

DOUBLE CHOCOLATE CHIP COOKIES

COCONUT MACAROONS

LEMON SQUARES

FRENCH MACARONS

Personal-sized, easy-to-handle, noncommittal, cookies are the median between a snack and a dessert. We might have a taste for something sweet but would likely turn down a traditional dessert—we don't feel like sitting down to a piece of cake or fancy tart; however, if a plate of cookies is available, we will most certainly grab one. Gladly. They're a mini-reward, a highlight to our day that lightens the mood.

And yet the sweet, delectable treats most certainly fall within the dessert category. Soft and chewy or crisp and light, cookies deliver the goods of a rich and satisfying taste. After a meal or as a midday pick-me-up, cookies can change the tone of an event, an encounter, or a special occasion. They're a social food, meant for sharing, and a carefully arranged platter of them will rarely escape a room without being emptied.

And then there's the kid factor. Long before Cookie Monster sang his classic *Sesame Street* song in 1972, children had been sneaking the treats out of Grandma's cookie jar for generations. Heidi has vivid childhood memories of entering her grandmother's home to the sweet aroma of cookies baking. Some of Grandma's favorite recipes have made their way to Croissants, appearing as sweet confections in the bakery case and attracting kids who have been allowed to stop for a special treat after school. Chocolate chip, molasses, lemon, or coconut, cookies make life a bit sweeter.

Roz's Chocolate Chip Cookies

THIS IS ANOTHER PERMANENT Croissants recipe handed down from its famous first baker, Roz. She had worked for years at the Dunes Golf and Beach Club, where her baking skills gained a wide reputation in a small town. When Roz came to Croissants, word traveled quickly around town that her sweets could now be had at the new bakery and café. Her secret to this recipe is the use of both margarine, which keeps the chocolate chip cookies from spreading too thin and browning too quickly, and butter, which delivers the perfect, rich taste.

MAKES 4 DOZEN COOKIES | PREP TIME: 20 MINUTES | BAKE TIME: 10 TO 12 MINUTES

8 ounces butter, softened

8 ounces margarine, softened

1 cup granulated sugar

1 1/2 cups brown sugar

2 eggs

2 teaspoons vanilla

4 1/2 cups all-purpose flour

2 teaspoons baking soda

1/4 teaspoon salt

3 cups semisweet chocolate chips

1. Preheat oven to 350°F.

2. Prepare cookie sheets by lining with parchment paper.

3. Blend butter with margarine until creamy. Add sugars. Add eggs one at a time. Add vanilla.

4. In a separate bowl, sift together flour, baking soda, and salt. Add to butter mixture. Stir in chocolate chips. Mix until just combined.

5. Scoop dough the size of a heaping teaspoon onto nonstick cookie sheet.

6. Bake 10 to 12 minutes, or until cookies are desired consistency. (I like to take them out a little early because I enjoy them soft.)

Croissants' Signature Brownies

RARELY REPLICATED ELSEWHERE, these decadent gems are also known as "kitchen sink" brownies. The classic question, "Do they have nuts?" is answered with, "Yes, and much more." The unusual ingredients here are pecans rather than walnuts, adding a Southern touch, and the addition of coconut, which results in an unexpected—and delicious—flavor profile. Chocolate chips round out the surprise ingredients, enhancing the chunky texture of the brownies.

MAKES 16 BROWNIES | PREP TIME: 20 MINUTES | BAKE TIME: 40 MINUTES

2 cups semisweet chocolate chips, divided

6 ounces butter

1 1/2 cups sugar

1/2 cup brown sugar

4 eggs, lightly beaten

1/2 cup all-purpose flour

1/2 cup chopped pecans

1/2 cup coconut

1. Preheat oven to 325°F.

2. Prepare a 9-by-9-inch baking pan by coating with nonstick spray.

3. Melt 1 1/2 cups of chocolate chips and butter together in microwave in 30-second intervals, being careful not to burn. Mix by hand with whisk. Mix in sugar and brown sugar using a spatula. Add eggs and mix. Add flour and mix.

4. Fold in pecans, coconut, and remaining chocolate chips to mixture.

5. Spread in pan and bake 35 to 40 minutes.

6. Cool and cut into 16 squares.

Lemon Squares

THIS RECIPE WAS a childhood favorite of Heidi's growing up in Pennsylvania, and the recipe was passed down by her mother. When Heidi and her brother would enter the house each day after school, they would guess what Mom had been baking. With Heidi's perceptive nose, she was usually right. Lemon Square days were the best days.

MAKES 24 SQUARES | PREP TIME: 20 MINUTES | BAKE TIME: 40 MINUTES

FOR THE CRUST:

1 pound unsalted butter, softened

1 cup powdered sugar

4 cups all-purpose flour

FOR THE FILLING:

6 tablespoons all-purpose flour

$1/2$ teaspoon salt

$3 1/3$ cups sugar

$1 1/2$ teaspoons baking powder

$1 1/2$ cups lemon juice

8 eggs

Zest of 1 lemon

Powdered sugar

FOR THE CRUST:

1. Preheat oven to 325°F.

2. Prepare a 13-by-18-inch baking pan by buttering the bottom.

3. Mix butter and powdered sugar with electric mixer fitted with a paddle attachment. Cream until combined. Add flour and mix until combined.

4. Pat mixture into the bottom of prepared pan evenly.

5. Bake about 15 minutes, until golden brown.

FOR THE FILLING:

1. Reduce oven temperature to 300°F.

2. Sift flour, salt, sugar, and baking powder together in a bowl.

3. Gradually add lemon juice. Add eggs, one at a time, until combined. Add lemon zest.

4. Pour mixture over cooled crust. Bake for 25 minutes, until set.

5. Let cool, cut into squares, and dust with powdered sugar.

Grandma Erb's Molasses Cookies

... OTHERWISE KNOWN AS AMERICANA. Heidi's maternal grandmother, who lived in rural Pennsylvania and was raised during the Great Depression, had neither the time nor the resources to run out to the store to pick up specialty items. So Grandma Erb would make inexpensive treats with the ingredients she had on hand, and her house was always full of the aroma of baking when the grandchildren would visit. Heidi passes on Grandma Erb's legacy by filling Croissants' cases with the traditional cookies of her childhood.

MAKES 4 DOZEN COOKIES | PREP TIME: 20 MINUTES | BAKE TIME: 12 TO 14 MINUTES

2 cups all-purpose flour

1 1/2 teaspoons baking soda

1 teaspoon cinnamon

1/2 teaspoon nutmeg

1/2 teaspoon salt

6 ounces butter, softened

1 cup granulated sugar, plus extra for rolling cookies

1 egg

1/4 cup molasses

1. Preheat oven to 325°F.

2. Prepare cookie sheets by lining with parchment paper.

3. Sift together flour, baking soda, cinnamon, nutmeg, and salt.

4. Cream butter and sugar in a separate bowl. Mix in egg and molasses. Gradually mix in dry ingredients until dough forms.

5. Roll dough into balls about the diameter of a half dollar. Roll in sugar. Place on cookie sheet about 2 inches apart.

6. Bake 12 to 14 minutes, until set.

Double Chocolate Chip Cookies

THIS RECIPE WAS ORIGINALLY a Croissants specialty item made during the holidays. The cookies were rolled in powdered sugar before baking, which gave the effect of the treats being covered in snow; this was a big hit on holiday cookie trays. In fact, they were so popular that guests began to request them throughout the year, so now they're a permanent item in the bakery case. Outside of the holiday season, the cookies are made without the extra powdered sugar, so guests can enjoy them year-round, yet they're still a special treat come winter.

MAKES 2 DOZEN COOKIES | PREP TIME: 20 MINUTES | BAKE TIME: 12 MINUTES

3 cups semisweet chocolate chips, divided

8 ounces butter, softened

2 cups granulated sugar

4 eggs

2 teaspoons vanilla extract

3 cups all-purpose flour

2 teaspoons baking powder

1 teaspoon salt

1. Preheat oven to 325°F.

2. Prepare cookie sheets by lining with parchment paper.

3. Melt 2 cups chocolate chips in a double boiler.

4. Cream butter and sugar together until smooth with electric mixer fitted with paddle attachment. Add eggs one at a time until combined. Add vanilla.

5. Sift flour, baking powder, and salt together and add to butter/sugar mixture. Add remaining 1 cup chocolate chips and mix until combined.

6. Scoop dough the size of a heaping teaspoon 2 inches apart onto prepared cookie sheets.

7. Bake 12 minutes, or until done.

Coconut Macaroons

THE DENSE, RICH TEXTURE of a macaroon, combined with sweet coconut and incorporated with almonds, makes for an elegant cookie. Heidi's mother made this recipe at Christmastime, and something about the treat suggests sophistication and special occasions. For variations on the recipe, add cocoa to the mix to make chocolate Coconut Macaroons, or dip half the cookie in melted chocolate for an extra-indulgent touch.

MAKES 3 DOZEN COOKIES | PREP TIME: 10 MINUTES | BAKE TIME: 20 MINUTES

$^1/_2$ cup egg whites (about 4 eggs)

2 cups sugar

1 $^1/_2$ cups chopped almonds

3 $^1/_3$ cups sweetened, shredded coconut

1 teaspoon vanilla

1. Preheat oven to 300°F.

2. Prepare cookie sheet by coating with nonstick cooking spray.

3. Beat egg whites until foamy with electric mixer with whip attachment. Add sugar gradually. Beat until stiff peaks form.

4. Fold in all remaining ingredients.

5. Scoop dough the size of a heaping teaspoon 2 inches apart onto prepared cookie sheet.

6. Bake 20 minutes.

French Macarons

NOT TO BE CONFUSED with the macaroon, the French macaron is an entirely different confection. The meringue-based cookies are light and airy, while the filling may range from marzipan to ganache to buttercream to jam. The cookies' colors run a gamut as well, spanning from pink to green to cream to brown—on a tray, they make an impressive spectacle. The versatility of the cookie is one of the reasons the macaron is Heidi's absolute favorite. In addition, the use of almond flour makes this cookie gluten free. Pastry Chef Heather Cameron and her baking team worked for almost a year coming up with a recipe that would stand up to the humid Southern climate, and now that they've developed their secret concoction, the French cookie is here to stay.

MAKES 2 DOZEN COOKIES | PREP TIME: 90 MINUTES | BAKE TIME: 30 MINUTES

FOR THE PASTE:

4 ounces almond flour

4 ounces confectioners' sugar

1 1/2 ounces egg whites (about 1 egg), at room temperature

FOR THE MERINGUE:

1 1/2 ounces egg whites (about 1 egg), at room temperature

4 1/2 ounces granulated sugar

2 ounces water

FOR THE PASTE:

1. Using a mixer fitted with a paddle attachment, combine all ingredients.

2. Place paste in a separate bowl and cover with plastic wrap.

FOR THE MERINGUE:

1. In a mixer fitted with a whip attachment, add the egg whites and begin to whip at low speed. Set aside.

2. Place sugar and water in a pot and heat to 245°F. Remove from heat and slowly pour sugar into mixer with egg whites while whipping.

3. Whip at high speed, adding sugar gradually until cool and medium peaks form.

FOR THE MACARONS:

1. Preheat oven to 275°F.

2. Prepare cookie sheets by covering with parchment paper.

3. Temper the paste by adding $\frac{1}{3}$ of the meringue to it. Then gently fold in the remaining meringue.

4. Immediately put mixture into a pastry bag with a round tip. Pipe circles about the size of a quarter onto cookie sheets.

5. Let cookies sit 30 minutes, until a skin forms on them.

6. Bake for 10 minutes, rotating pan after 5 minutes.

7. Let cool completely, then fill 2 cookies each with your favorite fillings. You can use ganache or any icing or jelly. The possibilities are endless.

ENCORE

COCONUT CUSTARD CAKE

PUMPKIN CHEESECAKE

TRIPLE CHOCOLATE MOUSSE

GRANDMA SCHREINER'S
CHOCOLATE LOG

BLUEBERRY AND RASPBERRY TART

ROZ'S CARROT CAKE

BLACK FOREST TORTE

KEY LIME TART

Sweet, indulgent, rich, and extravagant, cakes represent celebration. Whether it's a wedding, birthday, graduation, holiday, or date night, a homemade cake conveys love, attention, and commitment blended with just a touch of elegance.

Often the centerpiece of a special occasion, and much like the guest of honor, a cake serves to wow as well as delight the senses. Put simply, cakes show off. With their painstakingly crafted icing designs and last-minute flourishes, they're often out to steal the spotlight.

Cakes have been at the very heart of Croissants' operation ever since the first patrons entered the bakery to a beautiful display case of sweet confections. Layer cakes piled high with icing, traditional European cakes sprinkled with powdered sugar, and formal cakes encased in fondant each lie in wait for that particular patron who will gasp in delight upon viewing it. After that, it's only a matter of time until that cake becomes a focus for excitement and joy on a very special occasion.

However, the final verdict on a cake's quality derives not from its appearance but its flavor. A magnificent cake is even more pleasing to the palate than to the eye, and at Croissants, that is the ultimate goal. "My favorite thing to do in the kitchen is decorate cakes," said Heidi. "Not only do I want them to be beautiful, but I want it to be the taste that's remembered."

Coconut Custard Cake

CROISSANTS' ORIGINAL COCONUT CAKE recipe was a coconut-flavored cake with cream-cheese icing, until one evening when Heidi and her husband, Gary, ordered a similar dessert at a restaurant in Charleston. Gary loved that cake, so Heidi endeavored to replicate it for him. She decided to use a coconut custard filling typically used in a coconut cream pie to make the cake richer, and her experiment worked. It's been on the Croissants menu ever since, and it's still Gary's favorite.

MAKES 1 (9-INCH) CAKE | PREP TIME: 40 MINUTES | BAKE TIME: 20 TO 25 MINUTES

FOR THE CAKE:

$2/3$ pound unsalted butter

$2 1/2$ cups sugar

4 eggs

$1 1/2$ cups heavy cream

1 tablespoon vanilla

$1/4$ cup coconut cream

2 tablespoons coconut rum

$2 1/2$ cups cake flour

4 teaspoons baking powder

1 teaspoon salt

FOR THE COCONUT CUSTARD FILLING:

$1 1/4$ cups heavy cream, divided

4 teaspoons cornstarch

$1/4$ pound unsalted butter

$3/4$ cup sugar

$2 1/4$ cups sweetened, shredded coconut

$1/4$ teaspoon vanilla

FOR THE CREAM CHEESE ICING:

8 ounces butter, softened

1 pound cream cheese, softened

1 teaspoon vanilla

2 cups sifted confectioners' sugar

FOR THE ASSEMBLY:

Fresh shredded coconut or toasted coconut

FOR THE CAKE:

1. Preheat oven to 350°F. Prepare 2 (9-inch) cake pans by placing parchment paper circles on the bottom of each and covering sides of the pans with nonstick spray.

2. Cream butter and sugar together using electric mixer with paddle attachment. Add eggs one at a time, mixing after each addition. Scrape the sides of the bowl.

3. In separate bowl mix the heavy cream, vanilla, coconut cream, and coconut rum. Set aside.

4. Combine the cake flour, baking powder, and salt in another bowl.

5. Add the dry and wet ingredients alternately to the butter and sugar mixture. Mix on medium for 3 minutes.

6. Pour half of the batter into each of the 2 prepared pans. Bake for 20 to 25 minutes, or until toothpick comes out clean.

FOR THE COCONUT CUSTARD FILLING:

1. In small bowl mix 1 tablespoon of heavy cream and cornstarch with a whisk.

2. Melt butter in a saucepan over medium heat. Add remaining cream, sugar, and coconut. Heat until almost boiling.

3. Add the cornstarch mixture and continue to heat until thick, stirring constantly with a whisk. Add vanilla.

FOR THE CREAM CHEESE ICING:

1. Mix butter and cream cheese with electric mixer, adding cream cheese to mixture until smooth and creamy.

2. Add vanilla.

3. Gradually add sugar until mixture reaches desired consistency.

FOR THE ASSEMBLY:

1. Let cake layers cool completely. Cut each layer in half, making 4 layers.

2. Fill a pastry bag with cream cheese icing. Pipe a ring around 1 layer of the cake using a large, round pastry tip. Place 3/4 cup of the coconut custard filling in the middle of the cake and spread to the edges so that the icing holds in the filling.

3. Stack the next cake layer; repeat the process. Stack a third layer and repeat the process.

4. Stack a fourth layer and ice the top and sides with cream cheese icing.

5. Enrobe the outside of the cake with fresh shredded coconut or toasted coconut.

Triple Chocolate Mousse

THIS RECIPE IS AN ADAPTATION of a cake served at Latif's, a Myrtle Beach bakery that operated in the 1980s. Croissants' patrons requested that Heidi create her own version of the delectable item, so she substituted a pecan crust—more fitting for South Carolina—for the walnut crust of the original recipe. The best strategy for enjoying this cake? Include a bit of each layer in every mouthful to fully appreciate the various textures and flavors. Because the creation of individual layers is time consuming, it's best to spread out the steps: make the first three layers one day and complete the dessert the next day.

MAKES 1 (9-INCH) CAKE | PREP AND BAKE TIME: 1 TO 2 DAYS

FOR THE CRUST:

1 1/2 cups ground pecans

1/3 cup sugar

Dash salt

3 tablespoons melted butter

FOR THE FUDGE LAYER:

8 ounces semisweet chocolate chips

3 tablespoons butter

1 tablespoon light corn syrup

7 ounces heavy cream

FOR THE CHOCOLATE MOUSSE LAYER:

1/2 pound butter, melted

1 1/2 cups brown sugar

4 ounces semisweet chocolate chips, melted

4 eggs

FOR THE CHOCOLATE WHIPPED CREAM LAYER:

2 cups heavy cream, divided

8 ounces semisweet chocolate, coarsely chopped (can substitute chocolate chips)

FOR THE CRUST:

1. Preheat oven to 325°F. Prepare 9-inch springform pan by lining with parchment paper circle and spraying sides with nonstick cooking spray.

2. Add pecans, sugar, and salt to melted butter.

3. Press mixture into bottom of prepared pan.

4. Bake about 8 minutes, until set.

FOR THE FUDGE LAYER:

1. Heat chocolate chips, butter, and corn syrup in a double boiler until melted. Add heavy cream and whisk until smooth.

2. Pour into pan over top of the cooled crust layer. Keep in refrigerator while preparing the next layer.

FOR THE CHOCOLATE MOUSSE LAYER:

1. Beat butter and sugar with electric mixer. Let cool a bit.

2. Add chocolate and mix.

3. Add eggs one at a time and beat on high speed. Scrape bowl in between each addition. Mix until smooth and creamy.

4. Pour into pan over top of the fudge layer and freeze overnight.

FOR THE CHOCOLATE WHIPPED CREAM LAYER:

1. Place 1 cup cream in a small saucepan over medium heat. Heat until almost boiling.

2. Pour over chocolate and mix vigorously with wire whip until smooth to make ganache.

3. In mixing bowl, whip remaining cream until stiff.

4. Fold in chocolate ganache.

FOR THE ASSEMBLY:

1. Remove bottom three layers from springform pan.

2. Top with chocolate whipped cream layer.

3. Spread a thin layer of chocolate ganache on top.

Blueberry and Raspberry Tart

THE TERM "TART" DERIVES from the French *tarte,* used to refer to a pastry dish that can be filled with either sweet or savory ingredients. In Southern hands, this recipe may have manifested itself as a pie, but with Heidi's European background, the tart is the perfect expression of fruit and pastry. Heidi's mother would make this dessert when guests would come to their home for dinner, and she passed it down as a beautiful special-occasion treat. Best of all, the abundance of fruit in the tart makes it less filling than a heavier piece of pie or cake.

MAKES 1 (9-INCH) TART | PREP TIME: 20 MINUTES | BAKE TIME: 50 MINUTES

FOR THE PASTRY:

1 1/2 cups all-purpose flour

1/4 cup sugar

6 ounces butter

2 tablespoons lemon juice

FOR THE TOPPING:

1/4 cup all-purpose flour

3/4 cup sugar

1/4 teaspoon cinnamon

5 cups fresh blueberries, divided

FOR THE ASSEMBLY:

1/2 cup fresh raspberries

Confectioners' sugar

Real whipped cream

FOR THE PASTRY:

1. Preheat oven to 350°F.

2. Mix flour, sugar, and butter with pastry blender. When mixture is coarse, sprinkle with lemon juice. Mold with hands until it forms dough.

3. Press into a 9-inch springform pan.

FOR THE TOPPING:

Mix flour, sugar, cinnamon, and 4 1/2 cups of blueberries together in a separate bowl.

FOR THE ASSEMBLY:

1. Spread topping evenly over the pastry bottom.

2. Bake approximately 50 minutes, until bubbly.

3. Remove from oven and sprinkle with remaining 1/2 cup blueberries and raspberries. Sprinkle with confectioners' sugar when cool, and serve with a dollop of real whipped cream.

Black Forest Torte

THE NAME OF THIS CAKE originates not from the Black Forest mountain range in southwestern Germany, as generally believed, but from a specialty liquor distilled from sour cherries called Schwarzwälder Kirschwasser, which also hails from that region. Heidi first encountered this cake when she visited her Grandmother Schreiner in Germany as a little girl. Her grandmother made the recipe using a sponge cake, as she generally had the ingredients on hand in her pantry, but Heidi's version uses a more dense chocolate cake.

MAKES 1 (9-INCH) CAKE | PREP TIME: 90 MINUTES | BAKE TIME: 30 TO 35 MINUTES

FOR THE CAKE:

4 ounces semisweet chocolate, chopped

2 1/3 cups cake flour

3/4 cup unsweetened cocoa powder

1 1/2 teaspoons baking powder

1/2 teaspoon baking soda

1/2 teaspoon salt

1 cup warm coffee

1 cup buttermilk

1 1/4 cups unsalted butter, softened

2 1/4 cups granulated sugar

5 large eggs, at room temperature

1 1/2 teaspoons pure vanilla

FOR THE BING CHERRY FILLING:

2 cups pitted Bing cherries

1/2 cup granulated sugar

1/8 cup cornstarch

1/4 cup Kirschwasser

FOR THE CHOCOLATE WHIPPED CREAM:

2 cups heavy cream, divided

8 ounces semisweet chocolate, coarsely chopped

1 tablespoon Godiva Milk Chocolate Liqueur or crème de cacao (optional)

FOR THE WHIPPED CREAM:

1 quart heavy cream

$^1/_4$ cup sugar

$^1/_4$ cup crème de cacao

FOR THE ASSEMBLY:

Dark chocolate, shaved, for garnish

Maraschino cherries (dipped in chocolate, if desired), for garnish

FOR THE CAKE:

1. Preheat oven to 350°F. Prepare 2 (9-inch) cake pans by placing parchment paper circles on the bottom of each.

2. Melt the chocolate in double boiler. Remove from heat and let it cool to room temperature.

3. In a separate bowl, sift the cake flour, cocoa powder, baking powder, baking soda, and salt. Set aside.

4. In a separate small bowl, mix the coffee and buttermilk.

5. Beat butter with electric mixer until smooth and creamy. Add the sugar and continue beating until the mixture is fluffy. Scrape sides of the bowl as needed. Add the eggs, one at a time. Mix between each addition. Add the vanilla and mix to combine. Then add the melted chocolate and beat until smooth.

6. Alternate adding coffee/buttermilk and flour mixtures. Mix well between additions.

7. Spread evenly in pans and bake for about 30 to 35 minutes, or until a toothpick inserted in center comes out clean.

FOR THE BING CHERRY FILLING:

1. Place cherries in saucepan over low heat, cover, and cook for about 15 minutes.

2. In a separate bowl, mix sugar and cornstarch. Add gradually to cherries, stirring constantly.

3. Cook until thick. Add Kirschwasser.

FOR THE CHOCOLATE WHIPPED CREAM:

1. Place 1 cup cream in a small saucepan over medium heat. Heat until almost boiling.

2. Pour over chocolate and mix vigorously with wire whip until smooth to make ganache. (Optional: Add chocolate liqueur or crème de cacao.)

3. In mixing bowl whip remaining cream until stiff.

4. Fold in chocolate ganache, reserving $^1/_4$ cup to spread on top of final cake layer.

FOR THE WHIPPED CREAM:

1. Whip cream with an electric mixer until it begins to thicken. Add sugar gradually just as it is becoming thick.

2. Fold in crème de cacao.

FOR THE ASSEMBLY:

1. Let cake cool completely. Cut each layer in half, resulting in 4 layers. Place bottom layer on cake plate. Spread with chocolate whipped cream.

2. Add cake layer. Spread with Bing cherry filling.

3. Add cake layer. Spread with chocolate whipped cream.

4. Add cake layer. Spread top with chocolate ganache. Ice sides with whipped cream.

5. Garnish sides with shaved chocolate and top with Maraschino cherries.

Pumpkin Cheesecake

THOUGH IT'S AVAILABLE YEAR-ROUND, this dessert becomes particularly popular in the fall. Its pungent spices and creamy texture are combined with a gingersnap crust, making that taste of autumn even more prominent. In September and October and straight through the holiday season, this cake is in high demand throughout the Myrtle Beach area.

MAKES 1 (9-INCH) CAKE | PREP TIME: 40 MINUTES | BAKE TIME: 90 MINUTES

2 cups ground gingersnap cookies

1/3 cup unsalted butter, melted

1 1/2 pounds cream cheese, softened

3/4 cup granulated sugar

1/2 cup light brown sugar

3 eggs

1 (15-ounce) can pumpkin puree

1/4 cup heavy cream

1 teaspoon vanilla

1 teaspoon cinnamon

1 teaspoon ground ginger

1 teaspoon ground nutmeg

Real whipped cream

1. Preheat oven to 325°F.

2. Spray 9-inch springform pan with nonstick cooking spray. Encase the bottom and sides of pan with aluminum foil.

3. Prepare crust by mixing ground gingersnap cookies and butter. Press evenly along bottom of prepared pan. Set aside.

4. With electric mixer fitted with a paddle attachment, beat softened cream cheese until smooth and creamy. Add both sugars and mix until combined. Add eggs one at a time, scraping down the bowl with a spatula in between each addition. Add pumpkin puree, cream, vanilla, and spices. Mix until combined.

5. Pour cheesecake batter into prepared pan. Place pan on a baking sheet and place in oven on center rack. Carefully pour hot water into the baking sheet until filled to create a water bath.

6. Gently shut door of oven and bake for 15 minutes. Turn temperature down to 275°F and bake for another 1 1/4 hours, until set.

7. Turn off oven. Leave oven ajar by placing a wooden spoon between the door and wall of the oven. Let cheesecake cool down in the oven for about 30 minutes before removing. Refrigerate overnight.

8. Remove from pan and top with whipped cream.

Grandma Schreiner's Chocolate Log

THIS HOLIDAY CAKE is Heidi's take on the *bûche de Noël,* or yule log, a traditional French dessert. Just like many dishes handed down through generations of families, this recipe from "Oma" came with a story. Heidi's father told her that years ago in Europe, when kings would collect taxes and taxpayers had no money, the government would accept alternative currency. For example, in the winter months, many taxpayers would pay with wood to be used as fuel. One taxpayer had no wood, but he was a wonderful baker, so he paid his taxes with a cake that looked like a log. Heidi has her doubts about the tale's veracity, but she creates the delicious traditional cake just the same.

MAKES 1 LOG | PREP TIME: 40 MINUTES | BAKE TIME: 10 MINUTES

FOR THE CAKE:

9 eggs, separated

1 1/2 cups sugar

1 teaspoon vanilla

1 cup all-purpose flour

1/2 cup unsweetened cocoa

Powdered sugar

FOR THE CHOCOLATE WHIPPED CREAM:

2 cups heavy cream, divided

8 ounces semisweet chocolate, coarsely chopped

1 tablespoon Godiva Milk Chocolate Liqueur or crème de cacao (optional)

FOR THE CAKE:

1. Preheat oven to 350°F. Prepare a jelly roll pan with parchment covering the bottom.

2. Beat egg whites on low with electric mixer until foamy. Gradually add sugar while continuing to beat. Beat until whites are stiff and form peaks.

3. In separate bowl beat yolks and vanilla with whisk until smooth and creamy. Mix 1/3 of the egg whites with the yolk mixture until incorporated.

4. Pour remaining whites over yolk mixture. Sift flour and cocoa over egg mixture. Fold all together carefully. (Note: Oma always used her hands to mix the batter so she wouldn't break down the fluffiness of the egg whites.)

5. Spread batter in prepared pan. Bake approximately 10 minutes, or until toothpick comes out clean.

6. Remove cake from pan immediately and place on dish towel or cloth napkin sprinkled with powdered sugar.

7. Roll immediately. Let cool.

FOR THE CHOCOLATE WHIPPED CREAM:

1. Place 1 cup cream in a small saucepan over medium heat and bring to a simmer.

2. Pour over chocolate in a bowl and mix vigorously with wire whip until smooth to make ganache. (Optional: Add chocolate liqueur or crème de cacao.)

3. In mixing bowl, whip remaining cream until stiff.

4. Fold in 1/4 of the chocolate ganache, reserving the remaining for the assembly.

FOR THE ASSEMBLY:

1. Unroll cake and spread with chocolate whipped cream.

2. Roll back up and top by pouring the remaining ganache over the cake.

Roz's Carrot Cake

CROISSANTS' VERY FIRST BAKER, Roz Simmons, contributed this classic recipe to the restaurant's permanent repertoire way back in 1995. Heidi required a bit of persuading to put this item on the menu; she had never been a big fan of carrot cake, having been partial to more European pastries and cakes. However, Roz knew her Southern audience. She assured Heidi, "Honey, when you see the sales of this cake, you will *love* carrot cake." As usual, Roz was right; carrot cake became a number one seller and continues to top the list of patrons' favorites.

MAKES 1 (9-INCH) CAKE | PREP TIME: 40 MINUTES | BAKE TIME: 90 MINUTES

FOR THE CAKE:

4 eggs

2 cups sugar

1 1/2 tablespoons cinnamon

2 cups all-purpose flour

1 teaspoon baking powder

4 teaspoons baking soda

1/2 teaspoon salt

1 1/4 cups vegetable oil

1 teaspoon vanilla

1 1/2 pounds shredded carrots

FOR THE CREAM CHEESE ICING:

8 ounces butter, softened

1 pound cream cheese, softened

1 teaspoon vanilla

2 cups sifted confectioners' sugar

FOR THE CAKE:

1. Preheat oven to 350°F. Prepare 2 (9-inch) cake pans by placing parchment paper circles on the bottom of each. Cover sides of pans with nonstick cooking spray.

2. Beat eggs with electric mixer. Add sugar.

3. Mix cinnamon, flour, baking powder, baking soda, and salt in a separate bowl. Add to egg mixture.

4. Add oil, vanilla, and carrots. Mix well.

5. Divide into prepared cake pans.

6. Bake 90 minutes.

FOR THE CREAM CHEESE ICING:

1. Mix butter with electric mixer until creamy. Add cream cheese and blend until smooth and creamy. Add vanilla.

2. Gradually add confectioners' sugar until desired consistency is reached.

FOR THE ASSEMBLY:

1. Let cake cool completely. Cut each layer in half, making 4 layers.

2. Spread the first layer with cream cheese icing, stack the next layer on top, and repeat 2 more times. Completely cover top and sides with cream cheese icing.

Key Lime Tart

IN KEEPING WITH the Southern tradition, this recipe is a bit sweeter than the typical key lime pie … and the flavor has hit home with Croissants' patrons, as the recipe hasn't changed in two decades. If you prefer a more tart pie, use half sweetened condensed milk and half unsweetened, and opt for a meringue topping rather than whipped cream. However, do not substitute an alternate key lime juice—Nellie & Joe's is a tried-and-true ingredient here.

MAKES 1 (9-INCH) TART | PREP TIME: 10 MINUTES | BAKE TIME: 15 MINUTES

FOR THE CRUST:

1 cup ground graham crackers

1 tablespoon melted butter

1 tablespoon sugar

FOR THE FILLING:

$2/3$ cup egg yolks (about 10 to 12 eggs)

4 cups sweetened condensed milk

$2/3$ cup Nellie & Joe's Famous Key West Lime Juice

Real whipped cream

FOR THE CRUST:

1. Preheat oven to 325°F. Prepare 1 (9-inch) springform pan by covering the bottom with parchment and covering the sides with nonstick cooking spray.

2. Mix all ingredients together in a bowl. Press into the bottom of prepared pan.

FOR THE FILLING:

1. Beat egg yolks with electric mixer until smooth. Mix in condensed milk. Add juice last to prevent yolks from curdling. Mix until incorporated.

2. Pour into prepared springform pan.

3. Bake 15 minutes, or until set.

4. Cool completely. Top with real whipped cream.

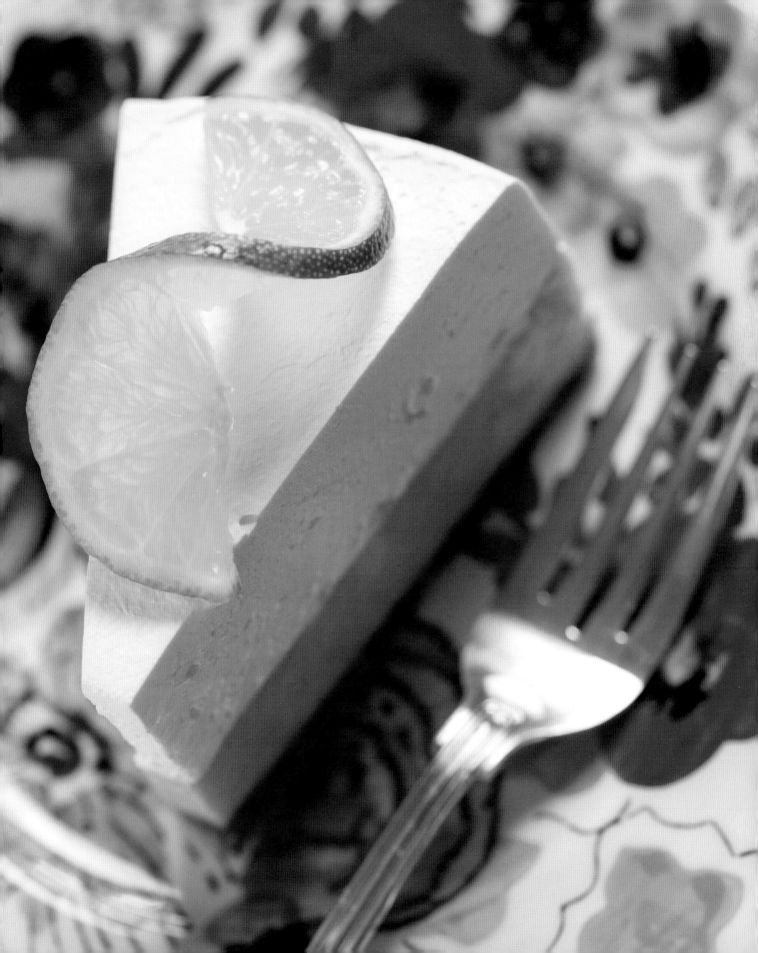

PANTRY

BACON AND TOMATO JAM	GRITS
BALSAMIC REDUCTION	HAM HOCK JUS
BEEF STOCK	MORNAY SAUCE
BEEF DEMI-GLACE	PIMENTO CHEESE
GOURNAY CHEESE	PEACH BBQ SAUCE
CHICKEN STOCK	TZATZIKI DRESSING
CLASSICO SAUCE	

A dish is only as strong as its weakest ingredient. Therefore the very best recipes are handcrafted all the way down to their stock, sauce, and spread. Croissants takes the time to simmer the ham hocks, boil the chicken, and stew the tomatoes to create the freshest bases for its dishes, and diners most certainly notice the attention to detail. While some recipes in this chapter are traditional, others display Croissants' unique flair for blending Southern and European tastes. These recipes are incorporated into items throughout the book, but they're also versatile enough to serve multiple purposes in a household pantry. Spread the Bacon and Tomato Jam on a fish sandwich for an added dimension of flavor; use the Chicken Stock instead of water to cook rice for added richness; serve Tzatziki Dressing as a dip for pita chips or vegetables. As the home kitchen becomes more centered on fresh foundations, creative cooks will continue to discover new, delicious uses for these basic staples.

Bacon and Tomato Jam

MAKES 2 CUPS | PREP TIME: 15 MINUTES | COOK TIME: 55 MINUTES

$^1/_2$ pound uncooked bacon, diced

$1\,^1/_2$ pounds fresh tomatoes, peeled, seeded, and diced

1 teaspoon minced garlic

1 teaspoon chopped fresh thyme

$^1/_2$ cup sugar

1 cup red wine

$1\,^1/_2$ cups red wine vinegar

1 teaspoon kosher salt

1 teaspoon ground black pepper

$^1/_4$ cup grenadine

1. In a large pot on low heat, add the diced bacon and slowly cook until crispy. Stir the bacon occasionally and cook until the majority of the fat is cooked off. Carefully drain grease from pot.

2. Add the tomatoes, garlic, and thyme and cook for 5 minutes.

3. Pour the sugar over the bacon and tomatoes and stir until dissolved. Add the red wine and red wine vinegar and simmer for 20 minutes.

4. Add salt, pepper, and grenadine and cook for an additional 10 minutes, or until the consistency of jam.

Balsamic Reduction

MAKES 1 CUP | PREP TIME: 5 MINUTES | COOK TIME: 15 MINUTES

2 cups balsamic vinegar

6 black peppercorns

1 sprig of thyme

1 shallot, thinly sliced

1. Place all of the ingredients in a small saucepan over medium heat.

2. Bring mixture to a boil.

3. Reduce heat and simmer until mixture reaches a syrup consistency, or until $1/3$ of liquid remains. (Note: The sauce will thicken as it cools, so be careful not to overreduce the vinegar.)

4. Pour through strainer.

Beef Stock

MAKES 2 QUARTS | PREP TIME: 30 MINUTES | COOK TIME: 2¹/₂ HOURS

6 to 7 pounds beef bones, preferably knucklebones

2 tablespoons olive oil

1 gallon water

Bouquet garni of parsley, sage, and thyme

1 carrot, sliced

1 stalk celery, sliced

1 turnip, sliced

2 large onions, sliced

2 cloves

2 bay leaves

1 tablespoon kosher salt

1¹/₂ teaspoons black peppercorns

1. Preheat oven to 350°F.

2. Place the bones in a roasting pan coated with olive oil.

3. Roast in oven about 30 minutes, until brown in color.

4. Remove from oven and place bones in a large pot.

5. Add all other ingredients. Bring to a boil slowly. Skim surface occasionally.

6. Continue cooking for about 1¹/₂ to 2 hours, or until stock is flavorful.

7. Remove bones from stock.

8. Strain stock, cool, and store.

Beef Demi-Glace

MAKES 3 CUPS | PREP TIME: 5 MINUTES | COOK TIME: 40 MINUTES

4 cups Beef Stock (facing)

2 cups red wine

Blend of your favorite herbs

1. Heat all ingredients in a large pot over medium heat.
2. Bring to a slow, steady boil.
3. Continue cooking about 30 to 40 minutes, until mixture thickens.

Gournay Cheese

MAKES 2 CUPS | PREP TIME: 10 MINUTES

6 ounces butter, softened

12 ounces cream cheese, softened

$1/4$ cup chives, finely chopped

$1/4$ cup garlic, finely chopped

$1 1/2$ teaspoons sea salt

1. Cream butter and cream cheese together.
2. Fold in remaining ingredients.

Chicken Stock

MAKES 2 QUARTS | PREP TIME: 30 MINUTES | COOK TIME: 2 HOURS

4- to 5-pound chicken, cleaned

1 gallon water

Bouquet garni of parsley, sage, and thyme

1 carrot, sliced

1 stalk celery, sliced

1 turnip, sliced

2 large onions, sliced

2 cloves

2 bay leaves

1 tablespoon kosher salt

1 1/2 teaspoons black peppercorns

1. Put whole chicken, including neck, with all other ingredients in a large pot. Bring to a boil slowly. Skim surface occasionally.

2. Continue cooking for about 1 1/2 to 2 hours, or until meat is tender and stock is flavorful.

3. Remove meat from liquid. (You can use the meat in another recipe.)

4. Strain stock, cool, and store.

Classico Sauce

MAKES 3 QUARTS | PREP TIME: 20 MINUTES | COOK TIME: 90 MINUTES

1 gallon peeled Roma tomatoes

2 yellow onions, diced coarsely

1 cup minced garlic cloves

1/2 cup chopped fresh basil, divided

1 1/2 teaspoons kosher salt

1 1/2 teaspoons black pepper

1/2 cup red wine

1 cup extra-virgin olive oil

1. Preheat oven to 350°F.

2. Combine all ingredients, except 1/4 cup basil and olive oil, in a deep baking dish. Cover with aluminum foil.

3. Bake for 1 hour. Remove foil and bake for 1/2 hour more.

4. Blend well with whisk, adding remaining basil and olive oil. If you prefer a smooth sauce, use an electric blender. This will need to be done in batches.

5. If making at home, you can portion into 1-quart (or smaller) freezer containers for later use.

Grits

MAKES 5 CUPS | PREP TIME: 5 MINUTES | COOK TIME: 45 MINUTES

2 quarts milk (or for creamy Grits, 1 quart milk and 1 quart real cream)

¼ pound butter

1 teaspoon salt

½ teaspoon pepper

2 cups grits

2 teaspoons finely chopped garlic (optional, for savory Grits)

2 teaspoons finely chopped shallots (optional, for savory Grits)

2 teaspoons finely chopped fresh thyme (optional, for savory Grits)

2 teaspoons olive oil (optional, for savory Grits)

1 cup Pimento Cheese (page 139) (optional, for Pimento Cheese Grits)

1. Bring milk, butter, salt, and pepper to a boil in medium saucepan. Be careful not to scorch.

2. Whisk in grits. Turn down to simmer. Cook for 40 to 45 minutes, stirring often.

For creamy Grits: Add real cream in the last few minutes of cooking.

For savory Grits: Add garlic, shallots, thyme, and olive oil before cooking.

For Pimento Cheese Grits: Fold in Pimento Cheese to prepared Grits.

Ham Hock Jus

MAKES 3 CUPS | PREP TIME: 30 MINUTES | COOK TIME: 60 MINUTES

2 tablespoons olive oil

3 ham hocks

3 yellow onions, chopped

3 carrots, chopped

3 celery stalks, chopped

Bouquet garni of thyme, sage, and bay leaves

3 cups red wine

$^1/_2$ cup port wine

2 cups Beef Demi-Glace (page 133)

Salt and pepper to taste

1. Heat olive oil in large pot. Add ham hocks and stir until they begin to caramelize.

2. Add vegetables and sauté until they begin to have a caramel color.

3. Add bouquet garni, red wine, and port wine. Bring to a boil and cook until mixture is reduced by $^1/_3$.

4. Add Beef Demi-Glace and simmer until mixture is reduced by $^1/_3$ and meat is tender.

5. Remove from heat. Remove hocks and season with salt and pepper.

6. Strain sauce, then store in refrigerator until use.

Mornay Sauce

MAKES 1 QUART | PREP TIME: 10 TO 15 MINUTES | COOK TIME: 20 TO 25 MINUTES

1 bay leaf

1 small onion

2 cloves

3 tablespoons butter

3 tablespoons all-purpose flour

1 cup whole milk

1 teaspoon fresh thyme

1 teaspoon kosher salt

1 teaspoon black pepper

1 cup grated Swiss cheese

1. Pin bay leaf on the side of the whole onion with cloves to make an onion pique. Set aside.

2. Melt butter in a saucepan over medium heat.

3. Add flour and reduce heat to low until it forms a roux.

4. Add milk, onion pique, and all remaining ingredients, except cheese. Simmer until sauce starts to thicken.

5. Remove onion pique.

6. Gradually add cheese, stirring constantly to avoid lumpiness.

Pimento Cheese

KNOWN AS THE "pate of the South."

MAKES 3 CUPS | PREP TIME: 20 MINUTES

8 ounces cream cheese, softened

1 pound cheddar cheese, shredded

$^1/_2$ cup mayonnaise

$^1/_4$ cup finely chopped onion

$^1/_4$ cup pimentos

1 teaspoon finely chopped garlic

1. In a large bowl, add softened cream cheese to shredded cheddar.

2. Add mayonnaise, onion, pimentos, and garlic.

3. Mix until incorporated. (Note: Be sure not to overmix, as mixture will turn mushy.)

Peach BBQ Sauce

MAKES 1 QUART | PREP TIME: 30 MINUTES | COOK TIME: 90 MINUTES

1 ½ teaspoons olive oil

1 small yellow onion, diced

1 teaspoon stripped and chopped thyme

1 tablespoon peeled and chopped garlic

1 (15-ounce) can sliced peaches in heavy syrup

½ teaspoon ginger powder

1 cup ketchup

¼ cup Worcestershire sauce

1 tablespoon molasses

¼ cup Jack Daniel's whiskey

1. Heat olive oil in a large pot over medium heat. Add onion.

2. Cook onion, stirring occasionally, until it begins to caramelize and turn brown.

3. Add thyme and garlic. Continue to cook for 3 to 5 minutes.

4. Add peaches, including syrup, and remaining ingredients. Simmer for 1 hour, or until the mixture begins to thicken.

5. Remove sauce from heat and allow to cool.

6. Pour cooled mixture into blender and blend until smooth.

Tzatziki Dressing

MAKES ¹/₂ CUP | PREP TIME: 1 DAY

1 cup plain yogurt

1 hothouse cucumber, peeled and seeded

2 teaspoons kosher salt

¹/₄ cup sour cream

1 ¹/₂ teaspoons champagne vinegar

1 tablespoon freshly squeezed lemon juice

1 ¹/₂ teaspoons olive oil

¹/₂ teaspoon minced garlic

Pinch black pepper

1. Place yogurt in a cheesecloth or paper towel and set over a bowl. Set aside.

2. Grate cucumber and toss it with salt. Place it in another cheesecloth or paper towel and set over another bowl.

3. Place both bowls in the refrigerator for about 4 hours to drain.

4. Transfer yogurt to a larger bowl. Squeeze as much liquid from the cucumber as possible, then add to the yogurt.

5. Add all other ingredients. Let sit in refrigerator overnight for best results.

THE FUTURE
of Food in
MYRTLE BEACH

The restaurant that Heidi built over the past two decades has evolved and grown at a complementary pace with the Myrtle Beach area. From a small beach town that attracted tourists from around the region, Myrtle Beach has developed into a national destination for leisure travel. Attracting visitors for its beaches, golf courses, fishing, outdoor adventure activities, and sports tourism, Myrtle Beach has made its mark as a fun, high-quality vacation spot.

As the scope of tourist activities in the area has expanded, so has the level and variety of culinary options; Croissants has been at the front and center of that movement. In its growth from a café and bakery into a Southern/European fusion bistro, Croissants has raised the bar for fine dining in Myrtle Beach through its creative dishes and incorporation of cutting-edge culinary style.

Heidi and her team continue to work toward enhancing the overall quality of food and dining in the area. Croissants holds special events throughout the year to bring the community together in celebrating a unique culinary heritage. Events such as the annual Spring Wine Tasting and Art Show highlight the finest of the area's specialty food, drink, and culture. The Fourth of July Cupcake Eating Contest takes place at the very height of Myrtle Beach's tourist season, providing visitors with a unique way to honor our nation's birthday. Locals eagerly await the Back to School Wine Dinner each September, as many parents share a toast to the return of school days for the kids. And October brings the spooky evening of Halloween and Croissants' Hallowine Dinner.

On a larger community scale, Heidi is a cofounder of the Coastal Uncorked Food, Wine, Beer & Spirits Festival. Together with local business leaders, she created the event as a means to build awareness of culinary opportunities in the Myrtle Beach area. The event, now operated by the Myrtle Beach Area Hospitality Association, celebrates its seventh year this spring and has grown to include a farm-to-table dinner, an oyster roast, and a mixology competition, in addition to dozens of smaller events that celebrate the unique, the talented, and the diverse in our area's food and drink industry. Regardless of the season, Croissants continually seeks out opportunities to share the enjoyment of fine cuisine both within its four walls and throughout the community.

In a tourist area where volume, quantity, and name recognition often allow chain restaurants to succeed over independent businesses, Croissants serves as a reminder that high-quality food combined with warm, welcoming service in an elegant atmosphere is a winning combination. Heidi has worked for years with other area restaurateurs to perpetuate and encourage the growth of independent restaurants in the Myrtle Beach area. David Brittain, both a colleague and close friend of Heidi and Gary's, was one of those industry leaders. He was particularly interested in and financially committed to the success of the culinary program at nearby Horry Georgetown Technical College. When David passed away suddenly in 2011, Heidi became inspired to continue his legacy of generosity. The Brittain family established the David L. Brittain Legacy Fund for Culinary Arts to raise funding for a new facility, the International Culinary Institute of Myrtle Beach at Horry Georgetown Technical College. The program has been developed to train chefs, provide them with opportunities to intern in local restaurants, and encourage them to stay in the area after graduation, thereby continuing to raise the dining standard throughout the community. Heidi is deeply committed to fundraising for this cause, and part of her campaign includes donating 10 percent of her cookbook profits to the program.

As Heidi continues to pursue her vision of Myrtle Beach as a culinary player on the East Coast, Croissants continues to serve up creative plates that reflect the twin traditions of European and Southern cuisines. Locals and tourists alike continue to visit, having their expectations regularly exceeded with inspired and surprising taste combinations. Y'all oughta come on in and see her.

Bonjour!

ACKNOWLEDGMENTS

There are many people who have made this book happen, and it would be impossible to mention them all. From relatives on both sides of the Atlantic, to the many talented chefs and bakers who have influenced and impacted recipes. Here are just a few:

To my wonderful husband, Gary, for his patience and confidence.

To Alexandra Eline, my sweet daughter, for coming up with the original organization for the book.

To all of the staff who have passed through the doors of Croissants to make it a hospitable and comfortable place for guests to enjoy their dining and fellowship experiences.

To the wonderful staff who have contributed their creativity in producing great-tasting food, including chef Bradley Daniels, pastry chef Heather Cameron, baker Roz Simmons, and chef Andrew Fortner.

To my amazing assistant, Kelli Lane, for always going above and beyond.

To my dear friends Jan and Carl Conrad, Ann and Rickie LeMay, and Jimmy and Ginny Ward for their support during this project.

To Brad Dean and the Myrtle Beach Area Chamber of Commerce for their support of the project.

To Will and Hatton Gravely for their continued support and friendship.

To Scott Brandon and his team at The Brandon Agency for their creativity in coming up with the slogan "Bonjour, Y'all!" however many years ago.

To Sara Sobota for her kind and eloquent words throughout the book.

To Scott Smallin for his artistic eye and his way of making the food want to jump off the page and onto your plate.

To Madge Baird and Bob Cooper at Gibbs Smith for having faith in the book and for their guidance on the project.

Last, but certainly not least, to all of our loyal customers who have made this culinary journey successful.

—Heidi Vukov

INDEX

Metric Conversion Chart

VOLUME MEASUREMENTS		WEIGHT MEASUREMENTS		TEMPERATURE CONVERSION	
U.S.	Metric	U.S.	Metric	Fahrenheit	Celsius
1 teaspoon	5 ml	1/2 ounce	15 g	250	120
1 tablespoon	15 ml	1 ounce	30 g	300	150
1/4 cup	60 ml	3 ounces	90 g	325	160
1/3 cup	75 ml	4 ounces	115 g	350	180
1/2 cup	125 ml	8 ounces	225 g	375	190
2/3 cup	150 ml	12 ounces	350 g	400	200
3/4 cup	175 ml	1 pound	450 g	425	220
1 cup	250 ml	2 1/4 pounds	1 kg	450	230